D1309364

913.04   179954
   H
Hibbert, Christopher
Treasures of the World: the
Popes.

William F. Laman Public Library
28th and Orange Streets
North Little Rock, Arkansas 72114

William F. Laman Public Library
28th and Orange Streets
North Little Rock, Arkansas 72114

THE POPES

TREASURES OF THE WORLD

THE POPES

by
Christopher Hibbert

STONEHENGE

Treasures of the World was created by
Tree Communications, Inc.
and published by Stonehenge Press Inc.

TREE COMMUNICATIONS, INC.

PRESIDENT
Rodney Friedman

PUBLISHER
Bruce Michel

VICE PRESIDENTS
Ronald Gross
Paul Levin

EDITOR
Charles L. Mee, Jr.

EXECUTIVE EDITOR
Shirley Tomkievicz

ART DIRECTOR
Sara Burris

PICTURE EDITOR
Mary Zuazua Jenkins

ASSOCIATE EDITORS
Thomas Dickey   Vance Muse   Henry Wiencek

ASSISTANT ART DIRECTOR
Carole Muller

ASSISTANT PICTURE EDITORS
Deborah Bull   Carol Gaskin
Charlie Holland   Linda Silvestri Sykes

COPY EDITOR
Fredrica A. Harvey

ASSISTANT COPY EDITOR
Todd C. Martin

PRODUCTION ASSISTANT
Peter Sparber

EDITORIAL ASSISTANTS
Martha J. Brown   Carol Epstein
Holly McLennan Wheelwright

FOREIGN RESEARCHERS
Rosemary Burgis (London) Sandra Diaz (Mexico City)
Eiko Fukuda (Tokyo) Bianca Spantigati Gabbrielli (Rome)
Mirka Gondicas (Athens) Patricia Hanna (Madrid)
Alice Jugie (Paris) Traudl Lessing (Vienna)
Dee Pattee (Munich) Brigitte Rückriegel (Bonn)
Simonetta Toraldo (Rome)

CONSULTING EDITORS
Joseph J. Thorndike, Jr.
Dr. Ulrich Hiesinger

STONEHENGE PRESS INC.

PUBLISHER
John Canova

EDITOR
Ezra Bowen

DEPUTY EDITOR
Carolyn Tasker

THE AUTHOR: Christopher Hibbert, a Fellow of the Royal Society of Literature, is the author of many biographies and historical works, including *The House of Medici: Its Rise and Fall* and *Days of the French Revolution.*

CONSULTANTS FOR THIS BOOK: *The Reverend L. Augustine Grady, S.J.*, is associate professor of theology at Fordham University. His special interest is in the theological background of Christian art. *The Honorable Edmund Howard,* for many years a member of the British diplomatic service, has been Counselor at the British Embassy in Rome and is the author of a history of Genoa.

© 1982 Stonehenge Press Inc. All rights reserved. No part of this book may be reproduced in any form or by any electronic or mechanical means, including information storage and retrieval devices or systems, without prior written permission from the publisher, except that brief passages may be quoted for reviews.
First Printing.
Published simultaneously in Canada.
Library of Congress catalogue card number 82-50155
ISBN 0-86706-024-7
ISBN 0-86706-047-6 (lib. bdg.)
ISBN 0-86706-048-4 (retail ed.)
STONEHENGE with its design is a registered trademark of Stonehenge Press Inc.
Printed in U.S.A. by R.R. Donnelley & Sons.
For reader information about any Stonehenge book, please write: Reader Information/ Stonehenge Press Inc./303 East Ohio Street/Chicago, Illinois 60611.

COVER: *Justin II, emperor of the eastern Roman Empire, gave this gem-studded, gold-and-silver cross to Pope John III in 570. Inside it, both pope and emperor believed, is part of Christ's cross.*

TITLE PAGE: *In this mosaic in Vatican City, an eighth-century pope, John VII, holds a model of a chapel he built. The square halo indicates that the portrait was done during his lifetime.*

OVERLEAF: *In a sixteenth-century fresco by Raphael, as Saints Peter and Paul appear overhead wielding swords, Pope Leo I rides out in 452 to beg Attila the Hun not to attack Rome. Attila spared the city.*

ABOVE: *This thirteenth-century statue of Christ seated on a throne originally stood upon the altar of Saint Peter's tomb. The copper statue is plated with gold and set with semiprecious stones.*

CONTENTS

ROME OF THE POPES

The popes have lived in Rome since the first century except for a sixty-eight-year interval in the fourteenth century, which they spent in Avignon, France. The map at right shows the main thoroughfares of modern Rome and the locations of important churches, residences, and other buildings associated with twenty centuries of papal history. The inset map shows in greater detail part of Vatican City, where popes have lived since the year 500, though not continuously. During the Middle Ages, for example, pontiffs resided across the Tiber at the Lateran Palace. Vatican City is a sovereign nation—at 109 acres, the smallest in the world—established in 1929 by a treaty between the Church and Italy.

KEY TO INSET MAP OF ST. PETER'S AND THE VATICAN PALACES

Three colors represent the approximate dates of construction of the buildings in the Vatican. The dark purple shows the outline of the original St. Peter's Basilica, built in the fourth century and razed in the fifteenth to make way for the present church. Light purple denotes thirteenth- to seventeenth-century buildings. The gold color shows buildings of the eighteenth to twentieth centuries.

The numbers indicate the following places:
1. Present St. Peter's Basilica
2. Sistine Chapel
3. Raphael's Stanze, rooms in the Borgia apartments painted by Raphael at request of Julius II
4. Raphael's Loggia, a gallery designed by Raphael and used by Leo X to house a collection of antiquities
5. Borgia apartments, rooms in a residential palace begun in the fifteenth century by Nicholas V and named for Alexander VI of the Borgia family
6. Bronze doors, built in 1618, at the entrance to the Apostolic Palace
7. Gallery of Maps
8. Gallery of Inscriptions, a collection of over five thousand pagan and Christian writings engraved in stone
9. Vatican Library
10. Courtyard of San Damaso
11. Courtyard of the Pinecone
12. Belvedere Courtyard
13. Tower of Nicholas V
14. Sacristy
15. Bernini's colonnade
16. Bernini's baldachin, or altar canopy
17. Pinacoteca, museum of art opened in 1932
18. Casina, or papal villa, of Pius IV
19. Scala Regia, monumental stairway by Bernini
20. Scala Pia, stairway built by Pius IX
21. Obelisk

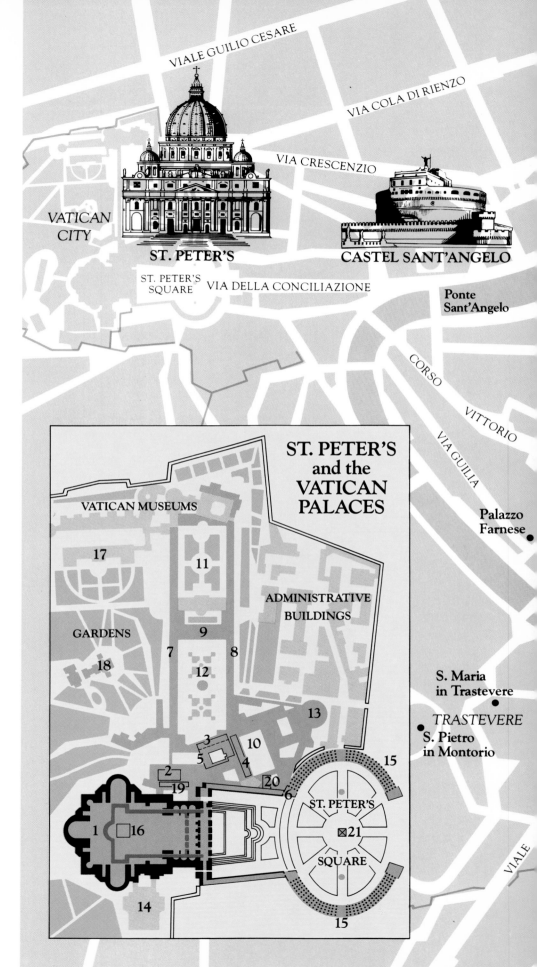

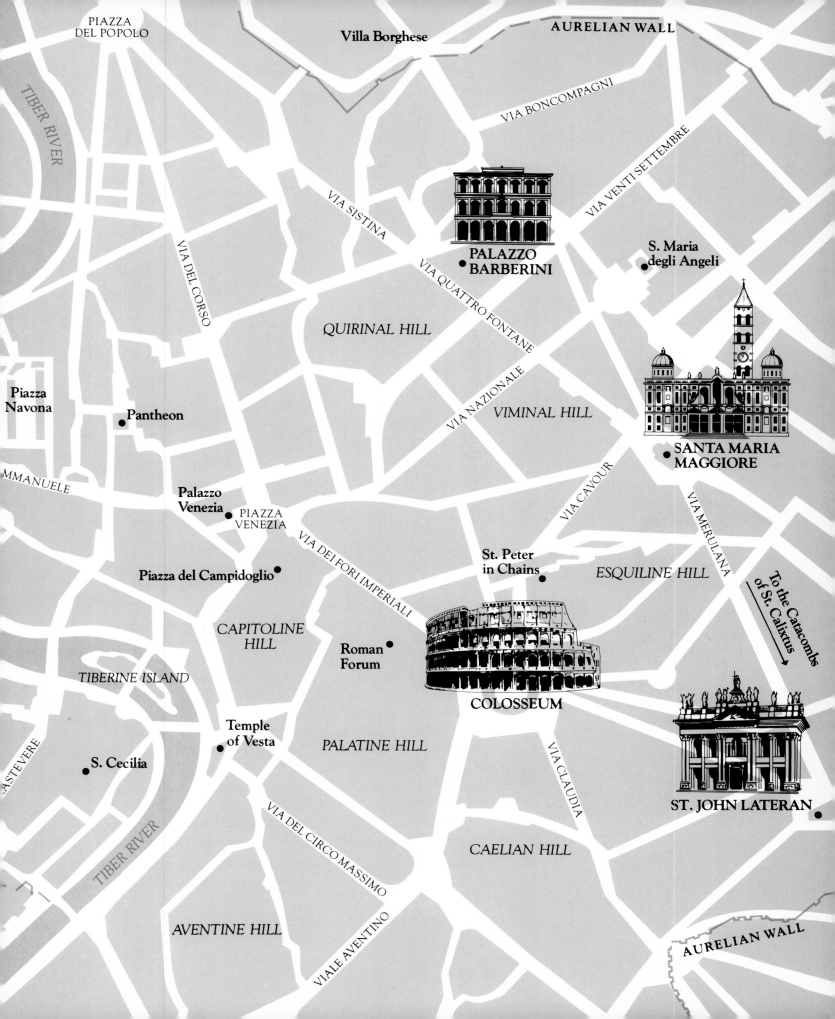

PIAZZA
DEL POPOLO

Villa Borghese

AURELIAN WALL

TIBER RIVER

VIA BONCOMPAGNI

VIA SISTINA

VIA DEL CORSO

VIA QUATTRO FONTANE

VIA VENTI SETTEMBRE

PALAZZO
BARBERINI

S. Maria
degli Angeli

QUIRINAL HILL

VIA NAZIONALE

VIMINAL HILL

SANTA MARIA
MAGGIORE

Piazza
Navona

Pantheon

MMANUELE

Palazzo
Venezia

PIAZZA
VENEZIA

VIA CAVOUR

VIA MERULANA

Piazza del Campidoglio

VIA DEI FORI IMPERIALI

St. Peter
in Chains

ESQUILINE HILL

To the Catacombs
of St. Calixtus

CAPITOLINE
HILL

TIBERINE ISLAND

Roman
Forum

COLOSSEUM

Temple
of Vesta

S. Cecilia

ASTEVERE

PALATINE HILL

VIA CLAUDIA

ST. JOHN LATERAN

TIBER RIVER

VIA DEL CIRCO MASSIMO

CAELIAN HILL

AVENTINE HILL

VIALE AVENTINO

AURELIAN WALL

I

THE FIRST MILLENNIUM

KEYS OF
THE KINGDOM

In the tenth year of the reign of the emperor Nero, a fire broke out in Rome, which the historian Cornelius Tacitus described as "more violent and destructive than any that ever befell" his city. "Furiously the destroying flames swept on, first over the level ground, then up the heights, then again plunging into the hollows, with a rapidity that outstripped all efforts to cope with them. The ancient city lent itself to their progress by its narrow tortuous streets and its misshapen blocks of buildings." When the fire was at last checked, after five days' raging, the government did all that it could for the distressed people, opening the imperial gardens to them, erecting temporary buildings, and distributing food. But the Romans hated their corrupt emperor and widely believed him to have been responsible for the calamity. They said that he had actually amused himself during the conflagration by singing to the music of his lyre. And so the emperor resolved to lay the blame elsewhere.

With this end in view he inflicted the most cruel tortures upon a people whom Tacitus described as "detested for their abominations

This third-century wall painting may be of Saint Peter, the leader of the Christian community in Rome until his martyrdom about the year A.D. 64.

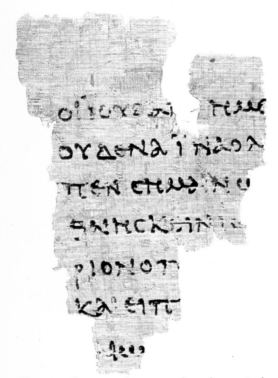

This second-century fragment of parchment is the oldest known manuscript of the New Testament. Its seven lines of Greek writing, from the eighteenth chapter of the Gospel of John, describe the trial of Jesus before his execution.

and popularly known by the name of Christians after one Christus who was put to death in the reign of Tiberius by the Procurator Pontius Pilate." Those who acknowledged themselves of this persuasion were arrested, and "their death was turned into a diversion: some were nailed on crosses; others sewn up in the skins of wild beasts, and exposed to the fury of dogs; yet others smeared with grease and used as torches to illuminate the darkness of the night." Nero used his own gardens for the spectacle and appeared among the crowd in the dress of a charioteer.

One of those who were martyred at about this time was Christ's own disciple, the fisherman Simon, to whom his Master had given the title of *petros* ("rock") and to whom he had said, "And I tell you, you are Peter, and on this rock I will build my Church, and the powers of death shall not prevail against it. I will give you the keys of the kingdom of heaven, and whatever you bind on earth shall be bound in heaven, and whatever you loose on earth shall be loosed in heaven." Peter held a position of divine, unique authority within the Christian community and had thus emerged as the leader of the earliest Christian Church, its first earthly father, its pope. After Peter was martyred, another vicar of Christ took his place, and then another. Believing their Church to be eternal, the Christians provided a way to select new leaders.

This early Christian Church, as Tacitus said, was checked for a time by Nero's persecutions, but soon "the detestable superstition broke out again." Emperor after emperor ordered persecutions of the sect—Domitian after Nero; then Trajan and Marcus Aurelius; Decius and Valerian; then, most terribly and over the longest period, Diocletian, the son of a liberated slave, who had been acclaimed emperor by his soldiers in 284. Faithful to his old Roman gods, Diocletian determined to rid the Empire entirely of the alien cult, which he saw as a threat to imperial unity as well as to his own divine status. Yet although he had thousands of Christians slain, their religion could not be suppressed. Forbidden to practice their faith in public, they resorted to meeting in the private dwellings of their fellow converts, while for the burial of the faithful they used the mazelike, subterranean galleries, passages, and niches that are called catacombs.

Dug out of the soft tufa rock that is found in abundance around Rome, these catacombs—from the Greek name for one of the tunnels—were not a Christian innovation. Indeed the practice of burying the dead in underground rock chambers had for centuries been common all over the Mediterranean world. But these Christian burial chambers in Rome, some forty of them extending over sixty miles beneath the roads leading out of the city, thereafter always took the name catacombs. In one of them the faithful laid the remains of Saint Peter—which were later moved to be buried under St. Peter's Basilica—as well as those of Saint Paul, who was also martyred in Rome, about A.D. 67. In another section, known as the catacombs of Saint Calixtus, after the third-century pope who managed it, several other leaders of the early Church were buried.

All the catacombs contained precious objects such as lamps and vessels of golden glass, relics of holy men, brave martyrs, and saints—in the early centuries sainthood came unofficially, by consensus of the faithful. The catacombs also became the repositories of the earliest Christian art, an art that displayed the faith in pictures in order to make it concrete and visible to the illiterate. From the beginning the paintings on the catacomb walls, the sculpture on the tombs, and the small furnishings, such as lamps and vases, followed the Roman style. But the subjects that the artists chose came from the Old and the New Testaments and expressed the hope of salvation and of union with God. Some of the early paintings were symbolic of Jesus—the good shepherd, the lamb, the fish—the Greek for which is formed acrostically by the initials for Jesus Christ, Son of God, Savior.

So over the years the catacombs became holy places. Hosts of pilgrims came to worship and to wonder at the marvels dimly discernible in the darkness. "When I was a boy receiving my education in Rome," wrote Saint Jerome in the fourth century, "I and my schoolfellows on Sundays used to make the circuit of the sepulchres of the apostles and martyrs. Many a time we went down into the

In 258, when ordered to hand over the Church's wealth, of which he was custodian, Saint Lawrence (above, in a twelfth-century mosaic) gathered the city's poor and sick and told officials, "Here is the Church's treasure." Roman authorities then burned him to death on a grill.

catacombs. They are excavated deep in the earth and contain on either side as you enter the bodies of the dead buried in the walls. It is all so dark there....You take each step with caution as though surrounded by deep night."

Before Saint Jerome's time the Christian Church in Rome had been frail and powerless, in constant danger of persecution or suppression. Yet at the beginning of the fourth century it had been transformed by the accession to the imperial throne of Constantine the Great, a Roman emperor and a Christian convert, who had fought his enemies under a Christian standard, declaring himself a champion of the faith. Constantine built the first basilica dedicated to Saint Peter. A basilica was a simple, oblong building with two rows of interior columns—a Roman architectural form the early Christians adopted. Constantine endowed his basilica with generous gifts of plate and property, and he also built the Constantinian Basilica on the site of what is now St. John Lateran, named for the grand Roman house of the Laterani family. (This church, rather than St. Peter's, was forever to be the cathedral of Rome, for it contained the official seat, or cathedra, of the pope, Rome's bishop.) Constantine gave the first palace of the Lateran, which had been part of his wife's dowry, to the leaders of the faith he protected. This palace now became the residence of the popes, and here, in their private oratory later to be known as the Sancta Sanctorum, they deposited the relics of the Church—reliquaries, crosses, and sacred objects.

Constantine died in 337, after having moved his capital to the eastern city he renamed for himself, Constantinople. The Roman Empire now had an eastern and a western half. The Church in Rome had begun to take shape as an indestructible force, the indissoluble organization that was to be the only institution to survive from the days of ancient Rome into our own. In 337 there had already been over thirty popes; and there were to be well over two hundred more. They were to display that astonishing variety of talent, incompetence, saintliness, worldliness, avarice, zeal, corruption, and unselfish honesty that characterized the papacy throughout its long history. They were the sons of peasants and noblemen, notaries and

In the fresco above, Roman Emperor Constantine offers a crown to Pope Sylvester I, seated at left, early in the fourth century. A Church legend tells that Sylvester refused the crown—a symbol of political authority over Western Europe—preferring to keep the humble ecclesiastical miter he wears here.

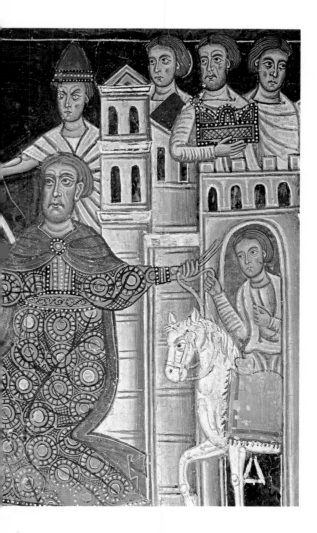

cobblers, soldiers and doctors. Some ascended the throne when they were old men, others when they were mere youths: Gregory IX was eighty-six; Benedict IX, eighteen. Some were scholars, others illiterate, some warriors, others peacemakers. Some were arrogant, some humble. Most were Italian but there were Frenchmen, too, among them, as well as Germans, Spaniards, Greeks, Dalmatians, Africans, Asiatics, a Dutchman, an Englishman, a Portuguese, and, most recently of all, a Pole. Some thirty of them were martyred; at least eighty are venerated as saints.

Yet diverse as they were in character and achievements, few were not conscious of their exalted position as guardians not only of the Church's spiritual supremacy but also of its temporal interests and its possessions: its places of worship and its treasures, treasures that reflected the moral force of the Christian faith.

Despite the papacy's lack of political power, this moral force ensured its survival through the barbarian invasions that convulsed Europe after the death of the emperor Constantine. The Goths invaded Italy about 410, the Huns in about 452, the Vandals in 455, the Lombards in 568. Yet ravaged as Christian places were, Christianity itself grew ever stronger as, from time to time, a pope appeared who combined spiritual zeal with inspiring leadership. One such pope was Leo the Great, elected in 440. The Roman Empire in the west was on the verge of disintegration, and in the east, bitter doctrinal disputes had divided Christendom. But Leo, maintaining that the popes were heirs to the powers of Saint Peter, went out unarmed against Attila, the dreaded leader of the Huns. Leo spoke to him with such forceful eloquence that the fierce, swarthy warrior who, according to a contemporary, "felt himself lord of all," turned back. And when Gaiseric, king of the Vandals, appeared with his savage host before the walls of Rome in 455, Leo did all in his power to induce him to restrain his men from murder, rape, and incendiarism when they plundered the city. Gaiseric did not keep all his promises, but his men at least spared the ancient basilicas.

After the departure of Gaiseric's troops, the papacy was generally recognized as a decisive factor in European affairs; and under its aegis

TEXT CONTINUED ON PAGE 22

IN THE CATACOMBS

Along the roads radiating from Rome, the city's early Christians mined over sixty miles of tunnels to serve as burial grounds. These catacombs—a word that derived from the Greek name for one of the tunnels—began as subterranean extensions of mausoleums in the third century, when land had become too scarce and expensive for surface burials. Gravediggers, like the one at left, extended the tunnels, excavated additional galleries in many levels below the early ones, and dug connecting passageways to form a vast underground network.

Contrary to legend the Christians never hid in the catacombs to escape the persecutions. In fact Roman authorities knew the locations of all the catacombs because cemeteries had to be registered with the government by law. Thus the catacombs would have been the worst hideouts.

Most of the catacombs were simple, unadorned tunnels resembling the one opposite. Wealthy Christians paid for the excavation of large rooms, spacious enough to accommodate relatives at memorial services. Gravediggers, who doubled as artists, decorated these crypts with lovely frescoes of people, animals, and episodes from the Bible that vividly symbolized the Christians' faith in deliverance from death.

Though some members of the Church were appalled by any religious images, which they took to be idolatrous, the Christianized Romans quickly set about making their faith visible to the naked eye. Here, on the walls of their crypts, Christian art was born.

In the tomb fresco above, probably painted in the third century, a gravedigger works, swinging his pickax in a catacomb lit by an oil lamp on the wall.

Simple tombs, known as loculi, line the high walls of the catacomb opposite. The earth outside of Rome was ideal for excavating such tunnels safely. It was made up of tufa—a material easy to clear away, yet strong and stable.

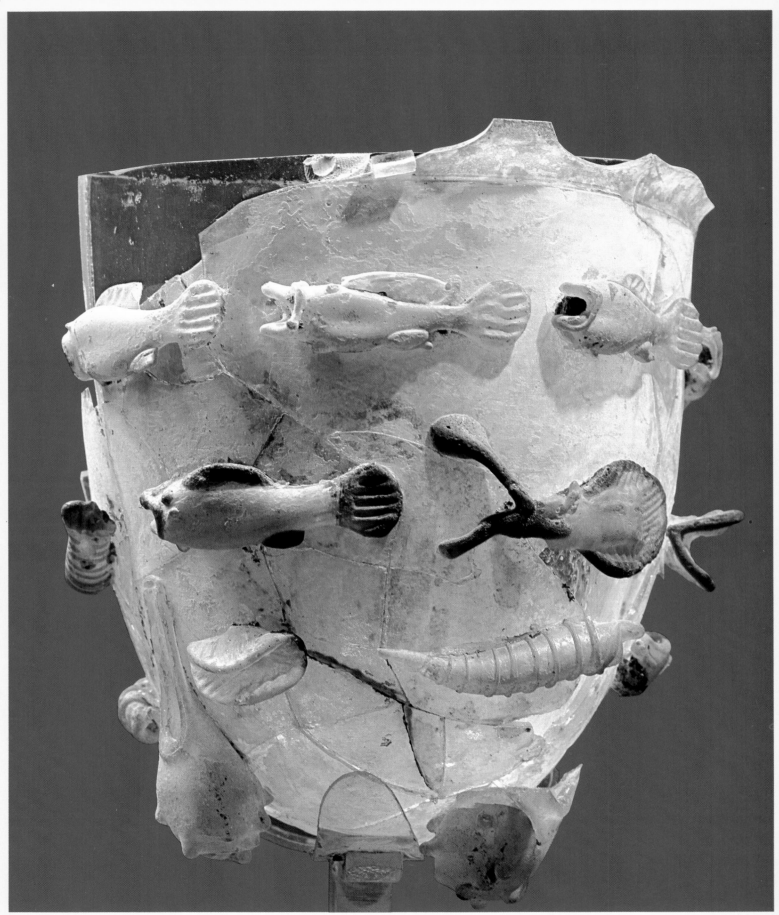

Three rows of sea creatures encircle the glass goblet above, made about 300, when the Romans still prized glass as a precious substance.

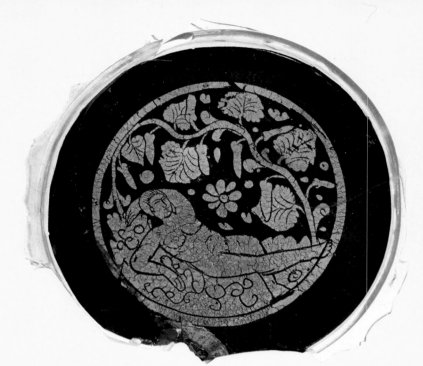

JONAH ASLEEP

When the early Christians laid a friend in his grave in the catacombs, they celebrated with a funeral feast—an old pagan custom imbued with a new Christian spirit. Death was an occasion for joy because the deceased was going to eternal rest with Christ. The glass goblet opposite, found in a catacomb, was in all likelihood used at a feast to toast the dead. The pieces of glass at right are the bottoms of other banquet vessels that mourners broke off and embedded in the mortar of tombs as markers to identify the deceased. The decorations in these glasses are cut from gold foil, which was then sandwiched between two layers of glass. Though these objects, called gold glasses, were made almost exclusively by Christian artists, pre-Christian subjects occasionally appear on them. At right the Old Testament prophet Jonah sleeps under a vine, and a Nereid—a sea nymph from Greek mythology—rides on a sea monster.

A GREEK SEA NYMPH

In the catacomb fresco at left, three heroes brave the flames of a furnace. During the captivity of the Jews in Babylonia, chronicled in the Old Testament Book of Daniel, King Nebuchadnezzar ordered these men, named Shadrach, Meshach, and Abednego, thrown into a furnace for refusing to worship the golden idol. They met the flames fearlessly, were kept safe by an angel, and emerged unhurt. Christians took heart from this story of faith overcoming persecution. Here the artist rendered the Jews with arms upraised, glorifying God for their deliverance.

Some three hundred representations of the good shepherd (left) appear in the catacombs. The image derived partly from a parable Christ tells in the Gospel of Saint Luke, about a shepherd who leaves his flock to find a single lost sheep—signifying Christ's concern with bringing even just one sinner back to the fold. To early Christians the figure of the shepherd had another significance. They believed Christ guided the soul of a Christian to paradise through regions fraught with demons, just as the shepherd here bears a sheep on his shoulders—an image from which the Christians took great comfort.

Candles illuminate a fourth-century painting (opposite) in the catacomb of Saint Calixtus, named for the deacon who managed it and later became a pope. The cross in the halo around the head indicates the figure is Christ himself. Through the passageway to the left of the painting is the crypt of the popes, where nine third-century pontiffs are buried. The catacomb of Saint Calixtus was the first cemetery officially established by the Christian community of Rome.

179954

William F. Laman Public Library
28th and Orange Streets
North Little Rock, Arkansas 72114

TEXT CONTINUED FROM PAGE 15

large numbers of converts were admitted into the faith, and numerous new churches were built. By the end of the fifth century there were already twenty-eight churches in Rome. After the foundation in 529 of Saint Benedict's monastery at Monte Cassino, monastic buildings also began to appear; and during the pontificate of the devout and universally respected Saint Gregory the Great, the "Father of the West," from 590 to 604, monks went out as missionaries into western Europe and across the Channel to England. As monasticism developed, so Christian culture spread, and the prestige of the papacy grew.

At the same time the temporal power of the papacy became more formidable. This came about in two ways: first because in the eighth century the people of Rome arose and drove out the representatives of the emperor in Constantinople and then organized their own government under the pope. The second cause of the increase in the temporal power of the papacy was the alliance Pope Stephen II, elected in 752, made with the Frankish king Pepin the Short against the Lombard invaders of Italy. Pepin gave the papacy large tracts of Lombard land in central Italy, which were to become the Papal States. The pope thus became a sovereign prince.

This alliance between the papacy and the Frankish kingdom was cemented when its throne was inherited by Pepin the Short's son, Charlemagne, a tall young man with arresting eyes who was vital, ambitious, hardworking, and masterful. He became ruler of almost all that is now France, Belgium, and the Netherlands as well as parts of Germany and Switzerland. On a visit to Rome, however, Charlemagne conceived an ambition for an even greater empire, a Christian empire to replace that of the Caesars, one that would stretch south of the Alps and beyond the Rhine to the Vistula, and would be a place of beauty, culture, and learning. On Christmas Day, 800, after celebrating Mass in St. Peter's, Pope Leo III placed a golden crown on Charlemagne's head; the Empire of the west was at last revived.

For a time, under the protection of the emperor, the Church prospered. But once the emperor died and could not provide it with

Bishop Maurice of Florence and two other men lose their heads to barbarian pillagers. The episode is legendary, but accurately reflects the tumult in sixth-century Italy, which Germanic and Byzantine armies turned into a bloody battleground.

the protection it required, the Church sank to a nadir of degradation that was the lowest in its long history. In 846 the Saracens from Arabia invaded Rome and pillaged St. Peter's. At the end of the century, the papacy, without the material forces to resist armed pressures, became a pawn in the hands of rival factions of the Roman nobility. Then the later German holders of the title of Holy Roman Emperor—never very satisfactory allies against the Roman barons—dominated the popes when they could.

Yet whenever the Church seemed in danger of dissolution, a strong pope would emerge to push papal claims of authority over other sovereign princes. Gregory VII, for instance, a great reforming pope elected in 1073, excommunicated the German king Henry IV, later Holy Roman Emperor. And when the emperor came to seek forgiveness and reinstatement, Pope Gregory, who was staying with his friend the countess of Tuscany at the castle of Canossa in northern Italy, kept him waiting for three days shivering in the cold outside the castle walls.

The papacy's quarrels with the Empire—and the kings of European nations—went on for centuries. Boniface VIII, elected pope in 1294, claimed full temporal and spiritual power for himself. In the bull *Unam Sanctam* (a bull carries the papal seal, or bulla, and is the pope's final word) he declared that "if the earthly power err it shall be judged by the spiritual power." Boniface dispensed excommunication after excommunication to gain obedience to his demands; but in so doing he enraged the powerful monarchs of the West and in particular King Philip IV of France. His legate in Rome attacked the pope at his palace and treated him so harshly that the pontiff died soon afterward, in October 1303.

Two years later a Frenchman, Bertrand de Got, became pope as Clement V and moved the papal residence from the Lateran Palace to Avignon, in the south of France. For sixty-eight years the French popes at Avignon, in what became known as the Babylonian captivity—in remembrance of the captivity of the nation of Israel in Babylonia—conducted the affairs of the Church. Rome, abandoned, sank into ruin and anarchy. In St. Peter's and in the Lateran

Pope Gregory (above, on the right) bestows a gift on Queen Theodelinda of the Lombards in 603. The queen had persuaded her tribe—Germanic barbarians who settled in northern Italy in the sixth century—to renounce their heretical beliefs and accept Roman Catholicism.

cattle grazed around the altars, and robbers roamed the streets.

The popes were not content to remain in France, but not until a remarkable young woman pleaded with Pope Gregory XI, the last French pope, did the papacy return to Rome, now to reside in the Vatican. This woman was the lively, passionate, illiterate daughter of a Sienese dyer, and she was to be canonized as Saint Catherine of Siena. But even after her pleas had been successful and the pope went back to Rome, the papacy was not safe. Gregory XI was succeeded by the zealous and austere Urban VI, whose overbearing manner and excessively sharp tongue raised so many enemies against him that a group of French cardinals declared his election forced and invalid. Thirteen out of sixteen French cardinals returned to Avignon and elected a new pope. Thus began the Great Schism, which, ravaging Christendom and inflicting great damage upon the authority of the Church, was not brought to an end until a new pope, Martin V, was elected in 1417 by a Church council convoked at Constance, Germany, by the Holy Roman Emperor.

The Great Schism was thus ended. Martin V reentered Rome, where he set out restoring the city's ruined churches, embellishing its other architectural masterpieces, and rehabilitating its works of art. This work was continued by Nicholas V, who was elected pope in 1447—a man of humble origin who had once worked in Florence as tutor in some of the cultivated families of that city and who dreamed of making Rome the cultural center of the world. Pope Nicholas was above all a bibliophile. Wherever he went he collected rare books and manuscripts, and eventually he was able to bequeath over a thousand Greek and Latin volumes to the Vatican Library. It became one of the greatest repositories in the world of medals, coins, and works of art, as well as of books and manuscripts.

The history of papal Rome itself as a repository of treasures had scarcely yet begun; but it was now to continue almost uninterruptedly for over five hundred years. The political problems of the papacy were far from settled, but the popes of the future—possessors and custodians of treasures—were also, by patronage of fine artists, to add to their ever-growing store.

THE HOLY
OF HOLIES

In the Sancta Sanctorum (above) a portrait of Christ stands on the altar, below which is the iron cage that, for centuries, held the Church's most sacred treasures.

In the entire world there is no holier place," says an inscription in the Sancta Sanctorum (the "Holy of Holies"), the popes' private chapel in the old Papal Palace of the Lateran in Rome. In this chapel, first used in the fourth century, the popes kept the most venerated relics of the Church: tunics worn by Saint Peter and John the Baptist; cloth dipped in the blood of martyrs; stones from the Holy Land; relics from the bodies of martyrs; and pieces of the cross on which Christ died. The stairs leading up to the chapel were taken from Pontius Pilate's palace in Jerusalem. Christ trod upon them on the day he was crucified.

To preserve and adorn the most sacred treasures of the faith, medieval popes commissioned the reliquaries on the following pages. In the course of centuries, these caskets of silver, gold, and enamel, and the fabrics that cushioned relics inside the containers, became hallowed objects themselves.

According to a Byzantine legend, one object in the Sancta Sanctorum—the portrait of Christ at left—arrived in Italy by divine intervention. In the eighth century when Christians in Constantinople opposed to the use of any religious images threatened to destroy the portrait, a bishop cast the image into the sea and it miraculously appeared in Rome. In 752 Pope Stephen II carried this portrait through the streets of Rome, praying for God's help in saving the city from invading Lombards.

The attacks of the Lombards, who ravaged the countryside around Rome and desecrated the catacombs, led the popes to remove the bones of martyrs from their tombs to the safety of churches inside Rome. Pope Paschal I, who reigned from 817 to 824, moved more than two thousand bodies, bringing the most important relics to the Sancta Sanctorum. It was Paschal who ordered the reliquaries on pages 30–35. The cloth on pages 36–37, on which Paschal laid a reliquary with pieces of the true cross, was one of the most precious fabrics in the world—silk from Constantinople.

The relics that Paschal I and other popes enshrined so sumptuously in the Sancta Sanctorum belonged to the saints whose souls were believed to be in paradise. Thus the sacred treasures on these pages—though they seem to be mementos of death—actually express an unwavering faith in eternal life.

An ornate silver casing (left) covers the portrait of Christ known as the Acheiropoietos—Greek for "not done by human hand." Saint Luke reportedly began to outline the portrait just after Christ ascended into heaven. He put it aside and later found that the image had taken on colors miraculously. The face visible here is a twelfth-century silk copy laid over the original to protect it. In the sixteenth century the keepers of the Sancta Sanctorum, the Brotherhood of the Company of the Most Holy Savior, attached medallions inscribed with their names to the wings of the angel on the case.

The brightly painted box at left, probably made in the ninth century, contains stones collected by a pilgrim in the Holy Land. The five scenes painted on the cover (detail, opposite) are, from bottom left, Christ's birth, baptism, crucifixion, resurrection, and ascension into heaven. Greek writing on two of the stones in the box says that they were gathered at Christ's birthplace in Bethlehem and from the area around his tomb.

The ninth-century silver box at right, embossed with scenes from the life of Christ, once held a reliquary, now lost, with a piece of the true cross. A Latin inscription around the central panel of the lid translates "Paschal, the overseer of the people of God, ordered [this] to be made," referring to Pope Paschal I. The Roman silversmith who fashioned the casket, eleven inches long, covered the raised portions of the scenes with gilt. The handle was added to the box later on, so that a pope or other high clergyman might carry the reliquary in processions.

The cross in the silver casket at left is the most precious treasure of the Sancta Sanctorum—beautifully decorated with enamel and once the repository of relics from the true cross. Pope Paschal I commissioned the reliquary in the ninth century. His successors carried it in processions on Good Friday, the day of Christ's death. On the lid of the box Saints Peter and Paul flank Christ, from whose throne four rivers flow through the Garden of Eden, symbolized by an engraved flower under the ring.

The enameled cross on page 33 and at left in detail is unusual because its central panel depicts an apocryphal story about Christ's birth. One of the midwives, to the right of the one washing the newborn Christ in the bottom of the central panel, wears a bandage on her arm: she had doubted that Mary was a virgin, and doubt caused her hand to wither. But she touched Christ's swaddling clothes, and her hand was healed. The early Church scholar Saint Jerome referred to this and other pious legends as nonsense. Pope Paschal, who commissioned the cross, apparently accepted the story.

This vivid swatch of silk cushioned the cross on the preceding pages. The cloth was chosen for its beautiful, albeit non-religious,

design. The dark spots on the neck and wings of the horse above were made by holy oil sprinkled on the cross by a pope.

CASKET CLOSED

Christ's disciple Simon appears in a brilliantly colored enamel medallion (opposite) on the lid of a silver and gold casket (at right, in two views) that was made by a Byzantine artist of the eleventh century. The Greek form of Simon's name is carved in gold on either side of his portrait. The casket is decorated with other enamels on its lid (in detail overleaf) and embossed on its sides with full-length portraits of four saints, among them (right, above) Saint John Chrysostom—an early preacher whose name means "golden mouth"—and the fourth-century saint Nicholas, the patron of children, whom folklore transformed into Santa Claus. Some time after the casket was made, the Church brought it to Rome to hold the head of a first- or second-century Roman woman, Praxedes, revered for centuries as a saint. Praxedes, according to early Christian legends, offered her house as a hiding place for Christians during persecutions, tended victims of torture, and buried martyrs. The relic in the casket has been worn down in places where thousands of devoted pilgrims have kissed it.

CASKET OPEN

In this enamel from the lid of the reliquary on the preceding page, the Virgin Mary and John the Baptist flank Christ, who is seated on a brightly colored throne. The highly realistic draping of the robes is an effect that only a master enamelist could achieve; but the maker of this small masterpiece is anonymous. All the enamels on the reliquary came from an earlier piece. Works of such superb quality were rare, and craftsmen were glad to reuse them.

II

PIUS II

THE POPE AS A RENAISSANCE MAN

During the hot summer of 1458, cardinals from all over Europe converged upon Rome to elect a new pope. Among them was an immensely rich and influential French cardinal, Guillaume d'Estouteville, archbishop of Rouen, who confidently expected to be chosen. When he arrived in Rome, d'Estouteville and his fellow cardinals were locked up in the apartments known as the conclave (from the Latin *cum clave*, "with a key") in accordance with a custom established in 1271 to hasten a papal election that had dragged on for almost three years. And here in these apartments, sleeping in private cells and meeting in a communal hall, the cardinals were required to remain until, by a two-thirds majority, they had agreed upon the man they deemed most worthy to occupy St. Peter's chair.

Intent upon occupying it himself, Cardinal d'Estouteville whispered promises of profit and positions of honor into eager ears in the latrines of the Vatican where, being the safest places in which to conduct intrigues, the meetings of the archbishop's supporters took

---

In a fresco by Bernardino Betti, known as Pinturicchio, "little painter," an enthroned Pius II canonizes Saint Catherine of Siena, whose body lies before him.

place. However, most of the cardinals favored not d'Estouteville but an equally ambitious Italian cardinal, who had been appointed bishop of Siena a mere two years after he had taken holy orders, and who was himself quietly confident of victory. And when the time came to count the votes, those cast in favor of the Italian did indeed outnumber his French rival's. But the majority was not sufficient. They had to resort to a roll call vote.

"All sat in their places, silent, pale, as though they had been struck senseless," recorded the cardinal of Siena in a dramatic account of the election that is part of his lively autobiography, or *Commentaries.* "No one spoke for some time, no one so much as moved a muscle of his body apart from his eyes which glanced this way, then that. The silence was astonishing." Suddenly the young Spanish cardinal, Rodrigo Borgia, stood up to declare, "I accede to the cardinal of Siena." But all fell silent once more. Two cardinals, afraid to vote openly, hurriedly left the room, "pleading the calls of nature." Then another one rose to announce his support of the cardinal of Siena. Even this did not secure the two-thirds majority: one more vote was wanted. Still no one spoke. At length the aged Prospero Colonna, a member of the Roman family to which Martin V had belonged, unsteadily rose to his feet. Cardinal d'Estouteville, a "slippery fellow who would sell his own soul," at least according to his rival, rushed to the old man's side and tried to propel him out of the room. Provoked by this, Colonna called out in loud protest, "I also accede to Siena, and I make him pope!"

The new pope was Enea Silvio de Piccolomini—known as Aeneas—the eldest of eighteen children of an impoverished nobleman who farmed his own land beyond the yellow stone walls of the small Tuscan village of Corsignano, between Siena and Perugia. As a child Aeneas had helped his father till the dry, gray, stony soil. The priest who instructed him found him an alert and responsive pupil, so the boy left home with his few possessions tied up in a bundle to complete his studies in Siena and afterward in Florence. He was a conscientious student, rising before dawn, laboriously copying out passages from books he was too poor to buy, then falling asleep over

The Holy Roman Emperor Frederick III meets his fiancée, Leonora of Portugal, at right, at an occasion presided over by the bishop of Siena. The bishop, Enea Silvio de Piccolomini—called Aeneas—who had been a secretary in Frederick's chancery, later became a cardinal and, in 1458, Pope Pius II.

his work at night, and once being woken from his slumbers by a burning nightcap set alight by an overturned oil lamp. Yet he found time, too, to enjoy himself with the friends he made so easily, to join them in picnics in the summer, in snowball fights in the winter, and at all times to make love to pretty girls who found his company enchanting. Babies were born, and he sent at least one home for his parents to bring up at Corsignano.

Charming, clever, amusing, and articulate, already a gifted poet and a persuasive orator, Aeneas had no trouble finding employment. In 1431 Cardinal Domenico Capranica, bishop of Fermo, invited him to become his secretary; the two men set out together across the Alps, "through mountains stiff with snow and ice that almost touched the sky," to Basel, Switzerland, where the cardinal had business to attend to at the council that had recently been convoked in the city by Pope Martin V. Here at Basel Aeneas came to the notice of Cardinal Albergati, an influential prelate, who sent him upon the first of his many diplomatic missions that he was to conduct with such skill.

Aeneas was to go to Scotland and persuade King James I to make raids across the border into England and thus keep English forces occupied in the northern counties. England, under King Henry VI, was at war with France—for the kings of England laid claim to the throne of France and had long been fighting to obtain it. The papacy was not eager to see the English unseat the French kings and hoped Aeneas might stir up a diversionary action. To the young Italian diplomat it was an exciting and hazardous adventure. Having narrowly escaped shipwreck in the stormy crossing, he landed at the Scottish port of Dunbar. Next he fulfilled a vow he had made to the Blessed Virgin by walking barefoot through icy tracks to the nearest shrine, ten miles away. Then he made his way to the court of King James, "a small, fat man, hot-tempered and greedy for vengeance."

In fact the wild Scots warriors raided the northern counties of England often enough, whether or not it suited papal purposes, but Aeneas apparently persuaded the king to send more. Then he traveled to England himself where, disguised as a merchant, he

As a young man in the employ of cardinals and kings, Pius II had worked in libraries like this fifteenth-century one—with its sharply canted desks, used to hold large manuscripts. A well-rounded scholar, Pius produced works on history, rhetoric, education, and biography.

sought shelter in the house of a peasant. The villagers regaled him with chicken and goose. In return he offered them wine and white bread, which he had obtained from a local monastery and which many of them had never tasted. The Englishmen then made their excuses and left for the safety of a stone tower where they were accustomed to take refuge from the Scottish raiders, leaving their women by the fire. No harm would come to *them*, they assured Aeneas, who observed, "They do not count rape as harm."

Two of these young women conducted their by now exhausted guest to a straw-filled room smelling strongly of goats and offered to spend the night with him there. Aeneas, too tired to accept and fearful that robbers might attack at any minute, sent them away. The next morning he left for London, where he learned that he had to apply for a royal permit to leave the country. Thinking that "it would be advisable not to do so," he set off for the coast to bribe the officials at Dover instead.

Changing masters as ambition suggested, he traveled widely on other missions, going to France and Switzerland as well as to Germany, where the emperor Frederick III, whom he served as secretary, crowned him imperial poet. And everywhere he went he showed that open-minded astuteness and adaptability, as well as that keen search for knowledge and lively interest in places, that were to make his *Commentaries* one of the most revealing of all Renaissance autobiographies. He was quick to detect and condemn the failings of his contemporaries. Of Cosimo de'Medici, the banker and patriarch of Florence and administrator of financial affairs of the Vatican curia, or government, Aeneas wrote that he was a cultured and knowledgeable man, "more lettered than merchants are wont to be." But Niccolo d'Este of Ferrara was a ruler "entirely given up to lust"; while Sigismondo Pandolfo Malatesta, master of Rimini, was the very "prince of all wickedness," the "poison of all Italy."

On entering the Church in 1446, Aeneas himself determined to put all sensuality behind him. "I do not deny my past," he told a friend; "I have been a great wanderer from what is right, but at least I know it and I hope the knowledge has not come too late." And when he became pope and chose the name Pius II, he wrote, "*Aeneam rejicite, Pium suscipite*"—"reject Aeneas, accept Pius." He tried to become a worthy occupant of his holy office. Yet he was as willing as many of his predecessors had been to promote the interests and indulge the expensive whims of his friends and family. And he retained the characteristics that made him so representative of early Renaissance versatility—curiosity and love of beauty.

His *Commentaries* vividly reveal the enjoyment he derived from the simple pleasures of the world, from eating alfresco in the beech woods of Monte Amiata, near his native Corsignana, from playing with a favorite puppy, or from watching his sister's baby at play—sometimes regretting, perhaps, that he had no legitimate offspring, for he loved children. Above all he delighted in the beauty of the Italian landscape, in its green woods and sparkling mountain lakes, in glades of asphodel and swallows' nests on rocky ledges, in blue fields of flax, yellow gorse on gently sloping hills, paths shaded by fruit trees, olives, and aged chestnuts, "rocky steps winding beneath vines to the water's edge where evergreen oaks stand between the cliffs, alive with the song of thrushes," and, around them all, the ruins of the past evoking memories of a distant, yet well-recorded and much-studied, age.

Steeped as he was in classical literature, Pius had a profound interest in the antiquities of ancient Rome and of the Roman Empire. Whenever he could he visited such remains, and he described them with infectious enthusiasm. In his zeal for constructing splendid new edifices he did not always behave as a true antiquarian might have. Though he forbade anyone to break up old columns, statues, and busts for mortar, he quarried marble from the Colosseum and the Roman Forum to build the marble steps leading up to St. Peter's. Yet when he decided to produce a monument worthy of the great classical tradition, Rome was not the site he selected. Instead, having hired the Florentine architect and sculptor Bernardo Rossellino, Pius went back to Corsignano to plan an entire new town. He intended to call it Pienza after his own papal name. Thus one of the most exquisite of all papal treasures—a whole town—was

TEXT CONTINUED ON PAGE 54

The cardinals of the Sacred Roman Rota, or high court of the Church, meet at their round table in an illumination of 1468. When Pius became pope, he declared that ultimate authority rested not with such courts or councils, but with the pope himself.

47

ARTICLES OF FAITH

The millennium called the Middle Ages—a thousand years from the bitter end of the Roman Empire, in the fifth century, to the beginnings of the Renaissance, in the fifteenth—was the long era of Christianization of Europe and the East. It was, too, one of the most creative eras of Christian art, when the bishops and the faithful of the Church commissioned painters, sculptors, illuminators, goldsmiths, carvers of ivory, and builders in stone to make both the articles of worship and the churches and cathedrals to hold them. Rome was the center of the growing Christian world, the primacy of the bishop of Rome as pope having been gradually established in Europe. But the ancient city and its accumulated treasures were more subject than most places to the discord of the times—to barbarian invasions, schisms, and fratricidal wars. After the German troops of Emperor Charles V sacked Rome in 1527, little remained of the magnificent inventory the Vatican and other Roman churches had amassed over the centuries. Of the precious few works that did survive, the altarpiece of the Last Judgment, opposite, dates from the eleventh or twelfth century and was once in the chapel of the Benedictine convent of St. Maria in Campo Marzio. It is signed at the bottom right of the circle with the names "Nicholaus and Johannes, painters." Nine and a half feet tall, it is one of the first, and finest, large-scale depictions of the Last Judgment in Western art.

In a detail from the altarpiece opposite, two women, riding on the backs of docile beasts, hold their children aloft. The women, who may have died in childbirth, appear here—at the Last Judgment—triumphantly reunited with their offspring. To their left in another variation on the theme of resurrection, fish and wild animals disgorge bits of human beings they had eaten during their lives on earth.

49

OUTER PANELS

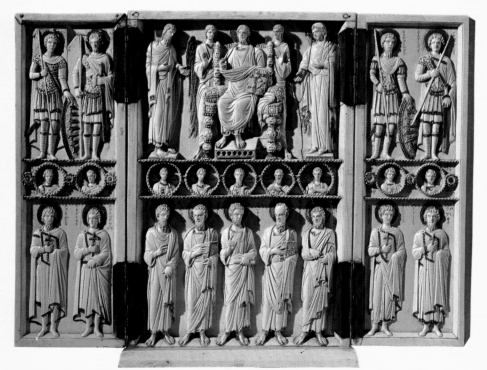

INNER PANELS

Less than a foot high and made as a tiny altarpiece, this three-paneled ivory, or triptych, of the tenth century—once painted and gilded—is the work of a Byzantine master. Its front panels, at bottom left, celebrate Christ on his throne (top center), flanked by Saint John and the Virgin, with the archangels Michael and Gabriel behind them. Various saints and soldiers stand in pairs in the wings. The back of the triptych, at upper left, has a cross set in the center panel and festooned with birds and flowers. Opposite, in a detail from the back of the triptych, John Chrysostom and Clement of Ancyra, two saints of the Eastern Church, are identified in Greek.

DETAIL FROM ALTARPIECE

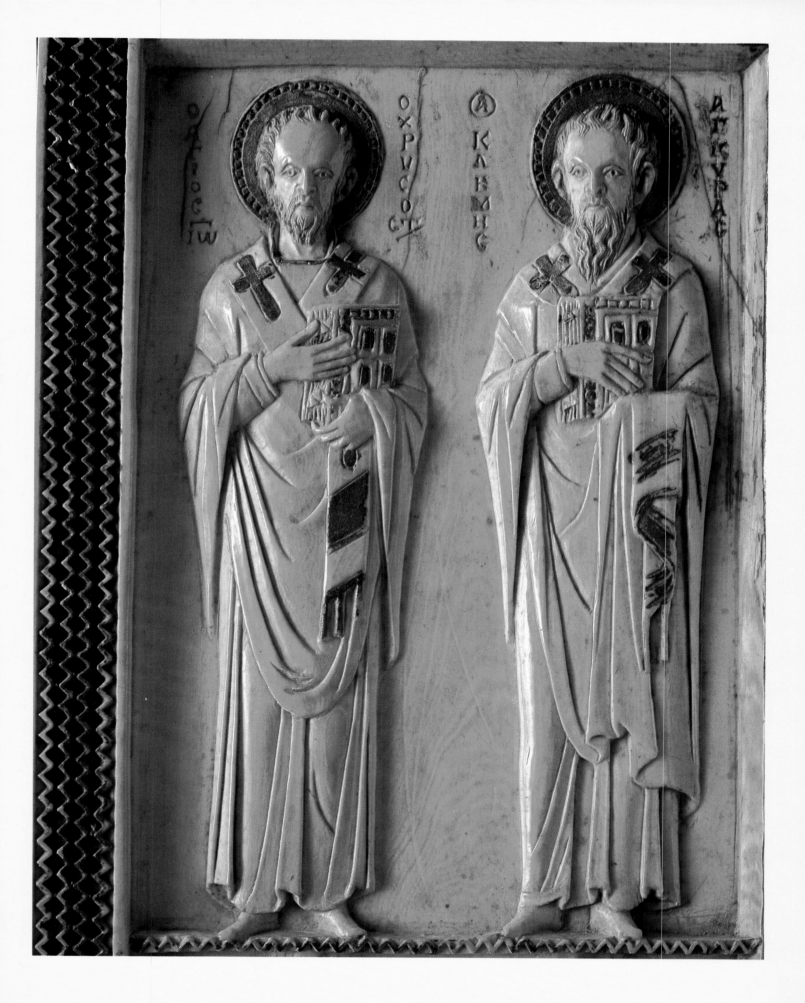

Giotto di Bondone, called simply Giotto, painted this altarpiece in the early fourteenth century. Commissioned by a cardinal who was a nephew of Pope Boniface VIII, the seven-foot-tall triptych once stood on the high altar of Old St. Peter's. Giotto, who lived from about 1266 to 1337, did more to determine the course of Western painting than any other painter had. Breaking from the formulas of Byzantine art, he gave his figures a firm, solid, worldly character, and so set the pace for generations of artists to glorify a human-centered universe. In the center panel of this triptych, the donor cardinal kneels at Christ's feet, his red hat lying before him. In the side panels Saint Peter is martyred at left, and Saint Paul is martyred—by decapitation—at right.

TEXT CONTINUED FROM PAGE 47

Turks defeat Christians (at lower right) in a battle on the Danube in 1396. The Turkish presence on the continent alarmed Europeans, and, in the next century, the Turks became the object of Pius's plans for what would be the last Holy Crusade.

destined to belong not to the papacy itself but to one man, Pius II.

Rossellino, one of the most accomplished sculptors of the time, had already worked on rebuilding St. Peter's, as well as on the Florentine Palazzo Rucellai, where his use of classical columns on the palace front was much to Pope Pius's taste. But while grateful for Rossellino's expert advice, Pius was anxious to supervise the planning of the new town himself. He knew exactly what he wanted: a cathedral, a bishop's palace, a larger, grander palace for himself and his family, a town hall, and summer residences for the officials of the papal court. The cathedral was to lie on the main axis of a piazza, to the east of which were to be the episcopals' and canons' palaces, to the west the Palazzo Piccolomini and its extensive garden with magnificent views toward Monte Amiata; and to the north, the town hall. The cathedral he wished to be modeled on a church he had admired in Austria, his own palace on the Palazzo Rucellai. The whole concept was to be one of the first examples of careful town planning since the days of ancient Rome.

And so it proved to be. The cost was tremendous: almost three times as much as the estimate that Rossellino had submitted; and when he was summoned to the papal presence he was consequently "in some apprehension." Yet Pius said to him, "You did well, Bernardo, in lying to us about the expense involved in this work. If you had told the truth you would never have induced us to spend so much money and neither this splendid palace, nor this church, the finest in all Italy, would be standing. Your deceit has built these glorious structures which are praised by all except the few that are consumed by envy. We thank you and think you deserve a special honor among all the architects of our time." He then ordered Rossellino to be paid his full fee and to be given a generous present as well as a scarlet robe. The relieved and grateful architect burst into tears.

Before his perfect little town was completed, Pius began to gather magnificent books and liturgical objects, splendid vestments, reliquaries, crosses, and tabernacles. Yet while enriching the treasures of the papacy by collecting these works of art, which unlike those holy relics of the Sancta Sanctorum reflected his taste as a cultured humanist and man of the world, he had never forgotten the mission he had promised to undertake at the time of his election—to persuade the Christian world to face its foreign enemies.

For years Pius had been urging Christendom to rise up in arms before "faith and learning [were] both destroyed" by the Turks. In 1453 these invaders had captured Constantinople and pushed their frontiers as far as the Danube River. To combat the menace Pius called upon all good Christian princes in Europe to meet him at Mantua to discuss a great crusade. Pius arrived at Mantua in splendid state, accompanied by twenty-six cardinals, each attended by troops of horsemen. Preceded by the servants and officials of the curia; by white, riderless horses caparisoned in gold; by noblemen in armor carrying banners displaying a cross, the keys of Saint Peter, and the five crescents of the arms of the Piccolomini; and by a golden tabernacle, came the pope. He himself sat high on his throne, wearing the papal robes, his miter blazing with precious gems. "From the gate all the way to the cathedral," Pius proudly recorded, "every foot of ground was covered with carpets and the walls on both sides were strewn with flowers and tapestries. Spectators crowded the windows and roofs and thronged the streets. In many places were altars smoking with incense. No voice was heard except the shouts of the populace crying 'Long live Pope Pius!'"

Yet despite this auspicious opening, the congress was a complete failure. Ruler after ruler made excuses not to take part: one was too old; another too preoccupied with unrest in his own country; a third was advised by his astrologers to stay at home; others were already at war elsewhere. Most of those who agreed to join in the crusade wanted compensation; and those who did not broke their promises. The envoys from the Holy Roman Emperor were so insignificant that the pope sent them home; England was represented by two obscure priests; the duke of Burgundy failed to arrive; so did the duke of Modena; the Venetians declined to do anything that might interfere with their trade in the eastern Mediterranean. The cardinals grumbled bitterly. As a contemporary wrote, "They said that Pius had been a fool to come to Mantua. . . . The place was marshy

Sultan Mohammed II (here in a sixteenth-century portrait), founder of the Ottoman empire, took Constantinople in 1453. In 1460, when Pius called for war against the Turks, he wrote Mohammed asking him—in vain—to convert to Christianity.

In the last of Pinturicchio's Sienese frescoes, the dying and disillusioned old warrior-pope arrives in Ancona, on the Adriatic, to lead a crusade he knows cannot be launched without allies to support it. On August 14, 1464, he was dead.

and unwholesome, everywhere was boiling hot; the wine was bad, and the food no better. Many were sick; a great number had fever and there was nothing to listen to but frogs."

Nevertheless the pope returned to Rome and declared his Holy War. Standing on the steps of St. Peter's, he displayed the pieces of skull of the apostle Andrew to the assembled multitude as he vowed to deliver the Christian world from its enemies. Ill as he was by then, racked with gout and fever, he set out on June 18, 1464, for Ancona, on the Adriatic coast, where the forces of Christendom were to convene. Carried to his barge on the Tiber and then across the Apennines in a litter, he knew that he was dying, and his attendants knew so too. From time to time they drew the curtains of the litter so that he could be spared the sight of his reluctant soldiers wandering off, having sold their arms to passing merchants. At Ancona there were but two ships to be seen in the harbor, and by the time a few others had sailed down the Adriatic from Venice, the pope was near death. During the night of August 14, he died, urging those around him not to draw back from the work of God, which he had begun. His words were in vain. Soon after his body had been taken into the cathedral, the Venetian galleys set sail for home and the cardinals returned to Rome to elect a new pope.

Pius II had failed to obtain the support of European princes for a crusade; the Turks inexorably advanced. In 1480 they even established a bridgehead in southern Italy by capturing the port of Otranto. Meanwhile another threat, more insidious than that of the Turks, endangered the papacy and its accumulating treasures. This was the menace posed by the growing extravagance and worldliness of the papal court.

Yet one of the paradoxes of the Renaissance papacy, as the next century was to prove, was that the most thorough-going materialism could bond with the strongest faith. In the palace and cathedral at Pienza, forgotten as future popes concentrated on beautifying the Vatican, the treasures of Pope Pius II—his sacred books, his reliquaries, his richly embroidered vestments—stood as testimony to that kind of bond.

A PAPAL CONNOISSEUR

Pius II's anulus piscatoris, or "fisherman's ring," once had his papal seal set on top. At his death, as custom required, the seal was broken and replaced by an amethyst.

The pope whose short papacy (1458 to 1464) falls at the border of two eras—just at the end of the Age of Faith and just at the beginning of the Renaissance—was himself a creature of both and a man with a strong and complex character. Known in his early, secular years as a humanist and a poet—and the only pope to write an autobiography—Pius in middle age embraced his faith purely and simply, and with near-mystical fervor tried to defend it in the last, doomed crusade. The artistic heritage he left behind in Pienza reflects both his modern humanism and his traditional spirituality—the pleasure in luxury of a poor boy who made good and the conscious restraint of a nobleman's son. Pienza, once called Corsignano, was Pius's birthplace, "a town of little repute but possessed of a healthful climate, excellent wine, and everything else that goes to sustain life," as he himself lovingly wrote of it. He transformed it into an architectural jewel, adding new palaces, a town square, and a new cathedral. So pleased was he with the result that in 1462 he issued a bull forbidding posterity to make any change in the decoration or floor plan of his church. In the museum of his cathedral is a collection of mostly small-scale, exquisite objects for liturgical use and devotional purposes, some of which he had made, while others are antiques he found and admired or even adapted to his taste. Taken all in all they reveal a pope who achieved, perhaps better than any other, the balance that the best popes always sought—between the life of the world and the life of the spirit.

On the front of Pius's miter, opposite, a Florentine work, the four enamels combine his pastoral and personal symbols. The Holy Ghost is at top, and Pius's papal coat of arms is at bottom. The remaining two enamels show the figures from the Annunciation: the archangel Gabriel, to the left, facing the Virgin, to the right.

Atop the pope's gold and silver crosier, or crook of office, the Virgin Mary and the archangel Gabriel kneel inside an enameled boat. Below them in a typical Renaissance flourish that unites pagan antiquity with Christianity, six columns support a classical temple.

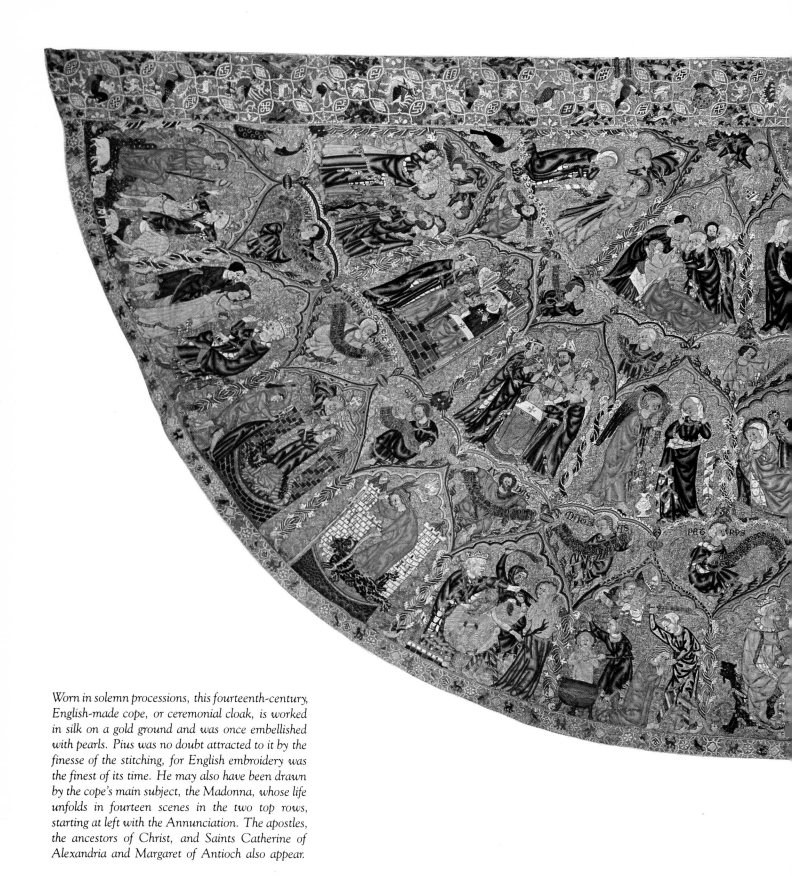

Worn in solemn processions, this fourteenth-century, English-made cope, or ceremonial cloak, is worked in silk on a gold ground and was once embellished with pearls. Pius was no doubt attracted to it by the finesse of the stitching, for English embroidery was the finest of its time. He may also have been drawn by the cope's main subject, the Madonna, whose life unfolds in fourteen scenes in the two top rows, starting at left with the Annunciation. The apostles, the ancestors of Christ, and Saints Catherine of Alexandria and Margaret of Antioch also appear.

OVERLEAF: *In details of two scenes from the cope above, an angel announces the birth of Jesus to a shepherd, at left, and the Magi adore the Infant on his mother's knee, at right. The embroiderer probably followed a design by a manuscript illustrator.*

Forty-four scenes from the life of Christ are carved into the foot-high boxwood cross and pedestal at right. Made about 1400, the carvings are in low relief in the base and nearly in the round in the cross. The crowning symbol is a pelican, which, with its legendary willingness to die, if necessary, to save its young, has become an enduring symbol of Christ.

The eight-inch-tall osculatory (from the Latin osculum, meaning "mouth" or "kiss"), opposite, was used during the celebration of the Mass. The osculatory would be kissed by the celebrant and then passed among members of the congregation for them to kiss. Pius's osculatory has a splendidly classical pediment, adorned with a horse and two non-Christian figures, signifying, perhaps, the obeisance that even the pagan world owed ultimately to Christ—whose crucifixion is rendered in silver below the pediment.

Oi le℟.

arma tu

a pha

re tră, et ar cum

et affer deuenatione tu

a ut co me dã.

Pius II bought this Book of Psalms, annotated in Gregorian chant, from Orvieto cathedral and commissioned several painters to illuminate it. Above, in the initial, stands David the psalmist,

who killed Goliath. On the right-hand page, Christ lays a crown on his mother's head. Pius II's coat of arms decorates the lower corners of both pages.

During Easter week of 1462, in lengthy and emotional public ceremonies and processions in Rome, Pius II received fragments of the skull of Saint Andrew the apostle. Christians had rescued the relic from its resting place in Greece before Turkish invaders overran the site, and the pope used it as a potent symbol of the need to raise a last crusade against the Turks. In his memoirs he describes leaving the skull in the Castel Sant'Angelo "to be kept till a proper receptacle could be prepared for it." The next year a Florentine goldsmith who worked in Rome produced the lifelike, thirty-inch-high reliquary, opposite, of silver with gold plate, pearls, over two hundred gems, and six large emeralds set on a bronze base. In the base, in detail at left, Pius's papal arms bear the crossed keys and the three-tiered crown of the popes above the Piccolomini cross with five crescents.

III

JULIUS II

THE WORLDLY VATICAN

The forty years following the death of Pius II had brought the institution of the papacy into decadence. Sixtus IV, for example, who built the Sistine Chapel, was a man of wild extravagance who lavished money and presents upon all his friends and relations. Innocent VIII, who succeeded him in 1484, used his pontificate to enrich his nephews and his illegitimate children. After him the cardinals elected possibly the most unworthy pope who ever reigned: Alexander VI, formerly Rodrigo Borgia of Spain. In the judgment of one historian of the day, Alexander's whole career was marked by "the most obscene behavior, insincerity, shamelessness, lying, faithlessness, impiety, insatiable avarice, inordinate ambition, cruelty worse than barbaric, and a most ardent cupidity to exalt his numerous children."

After three such popes as these, only the most remarkable man could save the papacy. And in October 1503 the coil of white smoke rising from the Vatican chimney—the traditional sign to the people of Rome that a new pope has been elected—was the first indication

---

This marble statue of Moses, which the great Renaissance artist Michelangelo carved for Julius II's tomb, bears a highly idealized countenance of the pope himself.

that such a man had been found. The man elected pope that day after one of the shortest conclaves in papal history was Giuliano della Rovere, the grandson of a fisherman from Liguria, in northern Italy. Giuliano kept his own name and became Julius II. Proud of his humble birth, he was much given to boasting of his poor childhood and liked to tell people how he had sailed down the coast with cargoes of onions. He was a tall, rough, impulsive, good-looking man, talkative, arrogant, and restless. "No one has any influence over him, and he consults few or none," the Venetian ambassador wrote. "Anything that he has been thinking during the night has to be carried out immediately. . . . Everything about him is on a magnificent scale, both his undertakings and his passions."

Julius had a fiercely commanding expression and a short temper. He always carried a stick, which he used to beat those who annoyed him, and he would hurl anything at hand, including his spectacles, at messengers who brought unwelcome news. He had had many mistresses in the past and had fathered three daughters after being created a cardinal. But he had thereafter displayed no interest in women. He enjoyed his food and drink to the full. He was no scholar, he used to say with defensive pride: he was more suited to the life of a soldier. When a sculptor asked him to suggest what should be placed in the hand of a statue of him, Julius replied, "Put a sword in it, not a book."

He had always been a man of the sword. As Cardinal della Rovere he had commanded the papal forces for Pope Innocent VIII, and he was determined to use the sword as pope to compel obedience to his rule in the Papal States. Local Italian princes had usurped some of these territories. Rival powers, such as Venice, had taken others. And Julius was resolved to reestablish papal rule in them all and to restore the temporal power of the papacy as essential to its authority. Soon after his election, therefore, with a strong force of cavalry and twenty-four cardinals in unwilling attendance, he rode north out of Rome, toward the cities of Perugia and Bologna, which had declared themselves free of papal jurisdiction. At his approach the leader of the Perugian rebels, Gian-Paolo Baglioni, took fright, surrendered,

In this portrait from the nineteenth century, Raphael lounges before his easel with one of his many mistresses, while Michelangelo lurks in the background. The scene is fanciful, but the rivalry between the two artists, both of them papal favorites, was real.

and knelt before him in humble submission. The pope forgave him, but added grimly, "Do it again and I'll hang you."

Baglioni nervously agreed to join the papal army as a condottiere—a mercenary. Giovanni Francesco Gonzaga, marquis of Mantua, also now joined the victorious forces. The pope then rode on with his enlarged army for Bologna, undeterred by the hardships of the march along the cold, rocky paths of the Apennines. The Bolognese rebel, Giovanni Bentivoglio, lost his nerve and deserted the city, and thus Julius entered Bologna in triumph in a brilliantly decorated palanquin.

Having dealt with Perugia and Bologna, he turned his attention to Rimini, Faenza, and Ravenna, which Venice had seized. In December 1508, declaring that he would join forces with anyone in order to reduce Venice once more "to a little fishing village," he allied himself not only with the kings of France and Spain, but also with the German emperor. This powerful alliance routed Venice's forces at Agnadello, in the province of Cremona, and the pope took his share of the spoils. But having made use of the French to extend the dominions of the Church, he now called upon all Italy to drive the French back beyond the Alps.

In personal command of his army, Julius marched north for Mirandola, where a French garrison was installed. Once more he was successful. He went about the camp in the bitter cold, his armor concealed by a white cloak, his head in a sheepskin hood, cursing his enemies, and moving his quarters when they were hit by cannon balls. Inspired by his restless energy, his men breached the walls of Mirandola. This fresh victory encouraged other cities to join the pope. Spain came to his aid against the French, while both Parma and Piacenza, abandoned by the French, declared themselves willing to join the Papal States. The pope annexed them immediately, announcing that he hated the Spanish quite as much as the French, and that he would not rest until they had been driven out of the peninsula too.

He returned to Rome in triumph. The Venetian envoy thought that never had any emperor or victorious general received so remarkable a welcome. A few thoughtful men, however, regretted that the vicar of Christ should resemble more the lion of Judah than the Lamb of God. The Dutch scholar Erasmus, himself an ordained priest, wrote ironically of the pope's entry into Bologna as though in Julius's own words: "Ah, would to God you had seen me borne aloft in Bologna! The horses and chariots, the marching battalions, the galloping commanders, the flaming torches, the pretty page boys, the pomp of bishops and glory of cardinals...and I borne aloft, head and author of all!"

Yet however much the warrior Pope Julius may have been, he was one of the most enlightened and discriminating patrons of art that the Western world had ever known. He had much of the Vatican Palace reconstructed and rebuilt the main courtyard, as well as the immense courtyard that stretches from the palace toward the Belvedere. Beneath its walls he laid out an extensive and lovely garden, the first great Roman pleasure garden since the days of the Caesars.

He hired artists as if recruiting an army—including all the great living masters of the Italian Renaissance. One of these was Raphael—in Italian, Raffaello Santi—who worked for the pope on the decoration of the new official apartments of the palace. Julius, refusing to live in the apartments of that "Spaniard of cursed memory"—Alexander VI—had decided to move to a higher floor. Raphael was complacent, unobtrusive, sweet-natured, and polite. The pope was delighted with him. The paintings in those lovely halls known as Raphael's Stanze proclaim the absolute power of Julius II, as well as the painter's genius. Julius commissioned Raphael to paint his portrait also; and, as the biographer Giorgio Vasari said, the result was "so true and lifelike that everyone who saw it trembled as if the Pope were standing there in person."

An even greater and more expensive undertaking of Julius's was the rebuilding of the ancient basilica of St. Peter's so that, as he said, it would "embody the greatness of the present and the future." To undertake this task, which he conceived as the premier monument to the everlasting glory of the papacy and the Church, he sent for

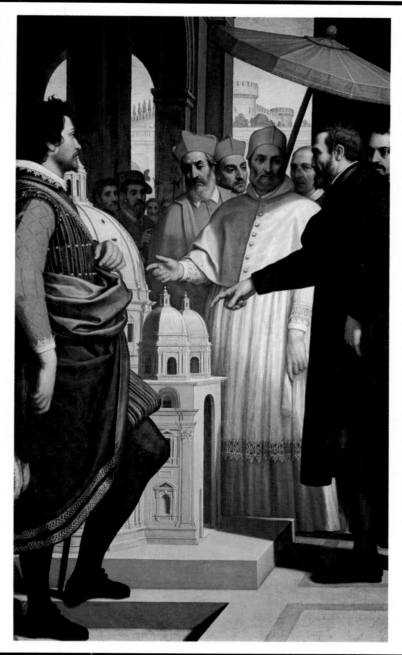

ST. PETER'S RENEWED

No project that Julius II initiated had a longer history than the new basilica built over Saint Peter's tomb. Julius's architect for the project, Bramante, designed a cross-shaped structure with four central piers supporting a dome, and this immense canopy evolved into the most ambitious architectural venture of its day. Work had not even begun on the dome when Bramante died in 1514, and Raphael—the next chief architect—worked on it only briefly. Then his successor Giuliano da Sangallo devised a far more elaborate structure for Pope Paul III, capped by a dome that fairly bristled with columns. Sangallo too died before his plan could be executed, and in 1547 the pope called upon Michelangelo, then age seventy-two. Treating the building almost as a sculpture, the master simplified the interior, added luminous attic windows, and made the outside more vertical, culminating in a dome crowned with a tall lantern. Still, construction lagged until 1558, when Pope Sixtus V, a pontiff as strong-willed as Julius II, finally had Giacomo della Porta carry out a scheme that embodied most of Michelangelo's conceptions. While the outer dome became more elliptic, the inner dome was just as Michelangelo had designed it—a perfect hemisphere rising 370 feet above the pavement. Completed in 1590, this dome inspired scores of others throughout the world, but the one above St. Peter's is often considered the greatest ever built.

In this seventeenth-century painting, Michelangelo, in black, presents a model of St. Peter's Basilica to Pope Paul IV—a rendering of the model Michelangelo made for the pope about 1560.

Donato d'Agnolo, called Bramante, who had arrived in Rome from Milan a few years before. The son of a well-to-do peasant, Bramante was then nearly sixty and had already designed buildings that profoundly influenced the architecture of the Renaissance.

Bramante set to work with a will, clearing the site of the decaying early medieval basilica with such eagerness that he became known as *mastro ruinante*, "master ruiner," and working hard on the designs of the structure that was to replace it. He settled upon a floor plan in the shape of a cross, with a dome to shelter the tomb of Saint Peter. This form and the drawings so pleased the pope that he ordered a medal to be struck depicting its elevation with domes and towers and a handsome portico. And on April 18, 1506, he accompanied a splendid procession to the site and climbed down into the foundation. Workmen set an earthen vase containing medals and coins in a small hole, and over this they lowered the white marble cornerstone, which read: "Pope Julius II of Liguria in the year 1506 restored this basilica which had fallen into decay."

Throughout Julius's pontificate the work on St. Peter's Basilica continued. Load after load of Carrara marble, Roman pozzolana (an ingredient of mortar), travertine from Tivoli, and lime from Montecelio was carted onto the site. One day he proudly remarked to an envoy who had also come to inspect the progress of the work, "Bramante tells me he has 2,500 men on the job. One could hold a review of such an army."

To pay for the expensive materials and workmen, Julius began granting numerous indulgences on a large scale—a practice that was to cause great trouble throughout the Church in the future. It was not a new idea: in exchange for a charitable donation, or other virtuous work, a sinner might have his time in purgatory shortened. At the same time Julius solicited contributions from all over Europe: the king of England sent tin for the roof, and the pope rewarded him with wine and Parmesan cheeses. After Bramante's death the work continued under successive masters, including Baldassare Peruzzi, Antonio and Giuliano da Sangallo, Raphael, and the most famous of all Julius's protégés, Michelangelo.

Soldiers of the Swiss Guard, a personal papal army established by Julius II, kneel during Mass in this detail from a fresco by Raphael. Julius recruited the mercenaries from Catholic cantons in Switzerland and had Michelangelo design their uniforms.

Early in his pontificate Julius had begun thinking of some monument appropriate for himself. Eventually deciding upon an immense marble tomb, he had sent for a young sculptor whose work in Florence had already set him apart as an artist of astonishing power. Michelangelo Buonarroti, the son of a poor Tuscan magistrate of aristocratic stock, was then twenty-nine years old, gloomy, taciturn, independent, and self-absorbed. Choosing to work in a locked room, unwilling to follow unquestioningly any brief or to undertake to finish a work in any given period, he was a most difficult man to employ or—with his touchy, abrasive temperament—even to like; but of his mastery of his craft there could be no doubt. And Pope Julius knew that if his tomb were to be the massive masterpiece he had in mind, Michelangelo must fashion it.

Michelangelo's own imagination was fired by the grandeur of the pope's ideas, and he produced a design that his fellow-Tuscan Vasari considered "an eloquent proof of his genius, for in beauty and magnificence, wealth of ornamentation and richness of statuary it surpassed every ancient or imperial tomb ever made." The tomb was to be a freestanding monument, thirty-six feet long and twenty-three feet wide, ornamented with some forty colossal statues. The magnificence of the concept of course appealed to Julius. He authorized Michelangelo to go to the famous quarries in the mountains of Carrara, where the sculptor spent eight months helping to excavate the great blocks of marble. Shipped by sea and river to Rome, they soon filled half the square of St. Peter's.

Back in Rome himself, Michelangelo set to work in a large room in Castel Sant' Angelo, the papal fort on the Tiber near the Vatican, to which the pope had a drawbridge built so that he could go over from time to time to see the marble taking shape. At first all went well; but then Julius's enthusiasm began to evaporate, and Michelangelo had trouble extracting any money from his patron. No longer did Julius visit the artist's studio; and when Michelangelo went to see Julius, the pope was not available. Fearful, as he told a friend, that if he stayed in Rome his "tomb would be built before the pope's," Michelangelo fled one night.

Lucrezia and Cesare Borgia were the likely models for the saint and the Roman emperor in this fresco detail from the Borgia apartments.

A DYNASTY OF WICKEDNESS

Among the Renaissance families who produced popes, none was more notorious than the Borgia, whose name became synonymous with corruption and murder by poison. The fear and hatred they aroused stemmed partly from prejudice against their Spanish origins and envy of the way they reached the top of Roman society—a process that began when Alfonso Borgia was elected Pope Calixtus III in 1455. But while some tales about Borgia cruelty were no doubt false, the clan's vices swiftly outpaced its virtues.

As a cardinal and then a pope, Rodrigo Borgia, Calixtus's nephew, fathered at least eight illegitimate children. He became Pope Alexander VI in 1492, probably by using bribery to defeat his rival, the future Pope Julius II, who was ever after an implacable Borgia foe. Shrewd and vigorous, Alexander was a greater patron of fortresses than of art, though he did commission some fine paintings by Pinturicchio (detail, above) for a suite at the Vatican called the Borgia apartments.

He also shamelessly used papal resources to promote his children, above all his favorites, Lucrezia and Cesare. He arranged for Lucrezia to wed a member of the wealthy Sforza family; then when she tired of her husband, Alexander coerced him into divorcing Lucrezia on the grounds that he was impotent. Her second husband, a prince of Naples, fared even worse. When the papacy broke with Naples, he was murdered—probably at the orders of Cesare, a man more ruthless than his father. In 1499 Cesare set out to establish an empire in the pope's name and seized most of the Papal States. He crowned his conquest by luring several treacherous officers to a castle, where he had them strangled. A brilliant

Alexander VI launched the Borgia's lurid reputation.

administrator, Cesare was probably the inspiration for Niccolò Machiavelli's famed discourse on power, *The Prince.*

Borgia power died with Alexander in 1503. Julius II, who was elected pope a month later, had Cesare arrested, and eventually the once-powerful prince was sent to Spain, where he died in 1507. But the political nature of the papacy was irrevocably changed, for Cesare and Alexander had shown that papal armies could firmly control the papal territories—a prospect that Julius II, the most martial of the popes, lost no time exploiting.

Once safely out of papal territory, he wrote curtly to the pope, "Since your Holiness no longer requires the monument, I am freed from my contract, and I will not sign a new one." Yet when the Florentine government informed the artist that they did not want to quarrel with the papacy over his defection, Michelangelo felt obliged to go back to him and humbly apologize. Julius was then at Bologna. The artist knelt before him, beseeching pardon and explaining that he had acted not from malice but from anger. The pope was at first unresponsive, keeping his head lowered and saying nothing. A cardinal who was present tried to make excuses for the penitent by explaining that he had erred through ignorance. The pope turned upon the prelate in fury, abusing him for being an ignorant rascal who could not comprehend the nature of artistic temperaments, and ordered him out of the room.

So he forgave Michelangelo and invited him to set to work again—not to return to the tomb as Michelangelo would have liked, however, but to cast in bronze a vast memorial statue of the pope, which, as the sculptor sadly commented, was "not his kind of art." Nevertheless, after a year's hard labor, he completed the statue—fourteen feet high and weighing six tons—and set it up on the facade of the church of San Petronio at Bologna. Within four years, however, the papal forces lost Bologna, and a mob brought the statue tumbling to the ground. The pope's enemy the duke of Ferrara had all but the head melted down and made into a cannon, which he named *la Giulia,* in derisive remembrance of Giuliano.

Having spent so long on so uncongenial a task, Michelangelo hoped that now Julius would allow him to return to Rome to resume his work on the tomb. But once again the pope required him to undertake a task that he felt ill-qualified to carry out—the painting of the ceiling of the Sistine Chapel. He protested that he had never so much as attempted a fresco before, that decorating a vault was an extremely difficult enterprise, and that he would make a mess of it. Yet the pope was insistent, and Michelangelo gave way. He looked up at the ten thousand square feet of ceiling and lunettes and felt dismayed.

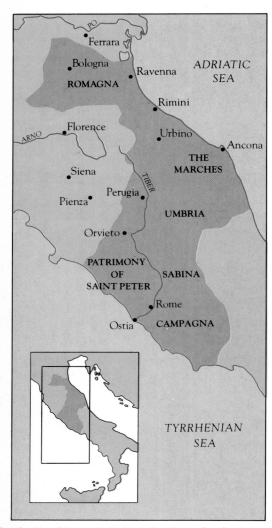

The Papal States in Julius's day formed a dominion encompassing most of central Italy and stretching from Romagna in the north to Campagna in the south. As temporal leader of these loosely knit cities and provinces, the pope was one of the most powerful princes on the Italian peninsula.

When he started work he found the labor physically, as well as emotionally, exhausting. He had to paint standing, looking upward for such long periods that his neck became so stiff and swollen he could not straighten it when he climbed down from the scaffold. In the summer it was stiflingly hot, and the plaster dust irritated his skin; in the winter, when the north wind blew, there was trouble with the mold. In all weathers the paint dripped down onto his face, his hair, and his beard. Repeatedly the pope interrupted him and belabored him—once even threatening to hurl him off the scaffold. But when at last on All Saints' Day, 1512, the work was done, the power and beauty of the paintings astounded everyone who saw them, and none more so than Pope Julius himself.

Now almost seventy and in his last year of life, Julius thought once more of his uncompleted tomb. It never reached the perfect state that he and Michelangelo had envisioned. But out of that grand conception one masterpiece came—the vibrant statue of Moses, one of the finest of all Michelangelo's works.

Age never mellowed Julius. To the end he was the *papa terribile*—the "terrible pope." As a sick old man he still spoke of waging a war to drive the Spaniards out of Italy. He was, indeed, a great patriot as well as a great patron; and, unlike so many of his contemporaries, he thought of Italy not as a mere collection of rival states but as an entity of its own. He was also a dauntless champion of the Church and of its capital city. The Romans, recognizing this, were deeply grateful. When he died in 1513, people wept in the streets and, according to the Florentine statesman and historian Francesco Guicciardini, "thronged to kiss his feet and gaze on his dead face, for all knew him to be a true Roman pontiff." Although "full of fury and extravagant conceptions," Guicciardini concluded, "he was lamented above all his predecessors and. . .is held in illustrious remembrance."

But the fame of this warrior-pope, who was the match of any prince of the sixteenth century, rested not upon his conquests but upon his collaboration with a sculptor who claimed he could not paint. Together they created a transcendent papal treasure—one of the most amazing artistic expressions of the Christian faith.

CREATING A
MASTERPIECE

Soft light illuminates the frescoed interior of the Sistine Chapel, whose capstone is a majestic, vaulted ceiling painted by Michelangelo for Julius II.

Io gia facto ûgozo ïquesto · steto
chome fa lacqua agacti ïlonbardia
over daltro paese chessi chesisia
chaforza luētre apicha soctolmēto

Labarba · alcielo · ellamemoria sento
ïsullo scrignio elpecto fo darpia
elpennel sopraluiso tuctauia
melfa gocciando ū richo pauimēto

E lôbi entrati miso nella peccia
e fo delcul p chotrapeso groppa
e passi sēza gliochi muouo ïuano

Dimāzi misalluga lachoreccia
ep piegarsi adietro sagroppa
e tēdomi comarcho soriano

Po fallacē estrano
surgie iliuditio chē lamēte porta
chē mal sipra p cerbodana torta

lamia pictura morta
difēdi orma giouanni elmio onore
nō sēdo ïlocg bō ne io pictore

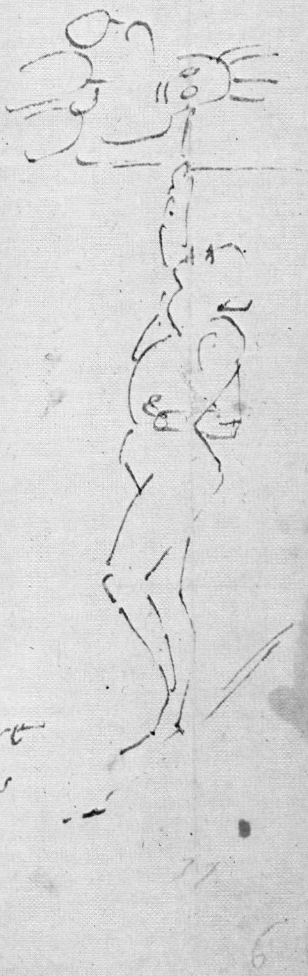

Of all the papal treasures, the greatest may be the Sistine Chapel. It was commissioned in 1473 by Julius's extravagant uncle, Sixtus IV, who had it built next to the Vatican. The Sistine has served, first and foremost, to house the cardinals during conclaves to elect a new pope, and both its architecture and decoration affirm the historic significance of this occasion. It has the dimensions of a church, with a central nave that is 130 feet long and 44 feet wide—measurements that correspond to those of Solomon's temple in the Bible. The floor is a mosaic of many-colored stones. A beautiful marble screen attributed to Mino da Fiesole, a sculptor of the early Renaissance, sets off the congregation's area from that reserved for the clergy. And girdling the walls is a series of frescoes, juxtaposing scenes from the lives of Moses and of Christ, executed for Sixtus by a group of fifteenth-century masters, among them Il Perugino, Piero di Cosimo, and Sandro Botticelli.

But the chapel's principal glory is the ceiling, a barreled vault sixty-seven feet above the floor, which Julius II decided to have painted as a memorial tribute to his uncle. The ambitious and cunning warrior-pope may also have timed the project to keep his favorite artist within easy reach. Whatever his motives the task itself was staggering. Yet the artist had almost no experience as a painter.

Michelangelo Buonarroti was thirty-three years old and widely admired as a sculptor when Julius first spoke to him about decorating the Sistine ceiling. The artist had recently completed a large-scale bronze statue of the pope and earlier had begun work on a colossal marble tomb for him. But he balked at Julius's request, insisting that painting was not his art and even proposing that his young rival, Raphael, be employed in his place. The more he refused, however, the more adamant and hot-tempered the irascible pontiff became, until Michelangelo reluctantly agreed. On May 10, 1508, for an advance payment of five hundred ducats, he began work—though he continued to express his frustration, as in the sonnet opposite, at taking on the monumental project.

The pictures on the following pages are selected drawings from those that Michelangelo made before and during the painting of the frescoes. Composed with pen and chalk, and sometimes as crowded with images as the ceiling itself, these preliminary studies reveal the artist's dreams and innermost visions: the private world of his creativity. Michelangelo must have produced hundreds of such studies, but he burned most of them toward the end of his life in an effort to erase any sign of the struggles he went through. Striving for perfection, he wanted the finished work to appear as if it had been perfect from the start.

He also seldom signed his drawings, and some that are attributed to him may in fact be copies drafted by his pupils. The ones in this portfolio, however, have come to be widely accepted as the master's. Even with the unfinished, exploratory quality that Michelangelo deplored, these surviving drawings are formidable works of art in their own right. And in arising almost spontaneously from his imagination, they provide an eloquent glimpse of steps leading up to the final work (pages 99–102): an overpowering masterpiece that secured lasting fame for both the artist and his patron.

At the end of a sonnet he composed about painting the Sistine ceiling, Michelangelo protests that "the place is wrong, and no painter I"—a recurring complaint he voiced about the pope's commission. The artist illustrated the poem, which is in his handwriting, with a caricature of himself at work on the vault. Rather than lying on his back, as legend has him doing, he stands upright as "my paintbrush all the day/doth drop a rich mosaic on my face."

Michelangelo's initial scheme for his frescoes is the subject of the sketch at right, a section of the Sistine ceiling lightly penned in ink; the artist later used the space at far right for several detailed studies of arms and hands in black chalk. Grappling with the chapel's architecture, he wanted a design that would join the ceiling to the frescoed sidewalls, and this first plan included—probably at the pope's behest—figures of the twelve apostles spaced among the tops of the windows. The curved central vault would be filled with conventional geometric forms. In the sketch one of the apostles sits on a throne between two window arches. Above the throne is a large square, set like a diamond, extending across the vault; the upper edge of the drawing ends where a throne on the opposite wall would appear. Almost immediately Michelangelo rejected the plan as too limited and rigid and convinced Julius II that "it was much too poor a thing to paint only the Apostles." In response the pope "bade me paint as I please"— possibly the first time a Renaissance patron granted an artist freedom of choice.

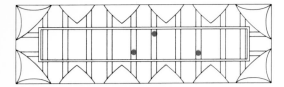

In the diagram of the Sistine ceiling, at left and on the following pages, a red dot marks the section to which each drawing in this portfolio corresponds. (Michelangelo discarded the plan on the preceding pages and the one directly below, so neither appears in the frescoes.) The entire Sistine vault, in color, is the foldout on pages 99–102.

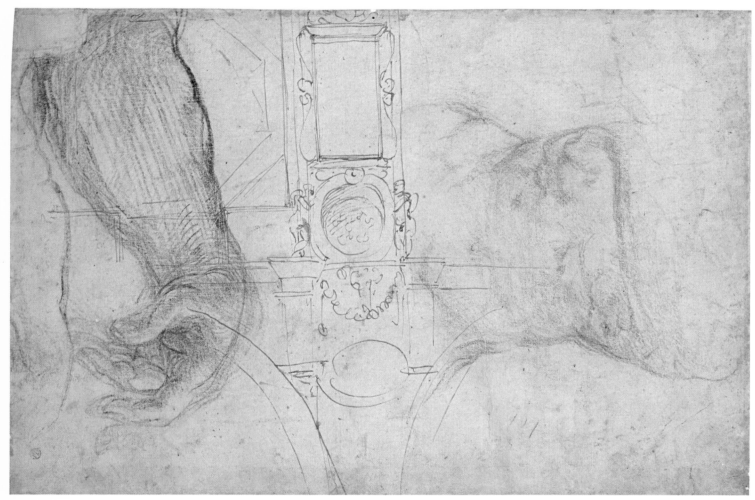

The middle sketch, similar in point of view to that on the preceding pages, is a more detailed but still unsatisfying plan organized around the apostles. This sheet also bears figure studies—of a massive left arm and, at right, a faint torso—that Michelangelo made after he began painting.

In rethinking how to fill his space, Michelangelo turned to what had been his most passionate concern as a sculptor: modeling the human body. Here he deftly sketched some ignudi, or nude youths, and these vibrant forms—three of which are connected to specific frescoes—would virtually explode across the ceiling. There was a long tradition of nudity in Christian art, which Julius completely accepted. However, Michelangelo created an unsurpassed variety of poses and expressions in his ignudi, using them to convey his deepest feelings about beauty and about man's nature and his relation to God.

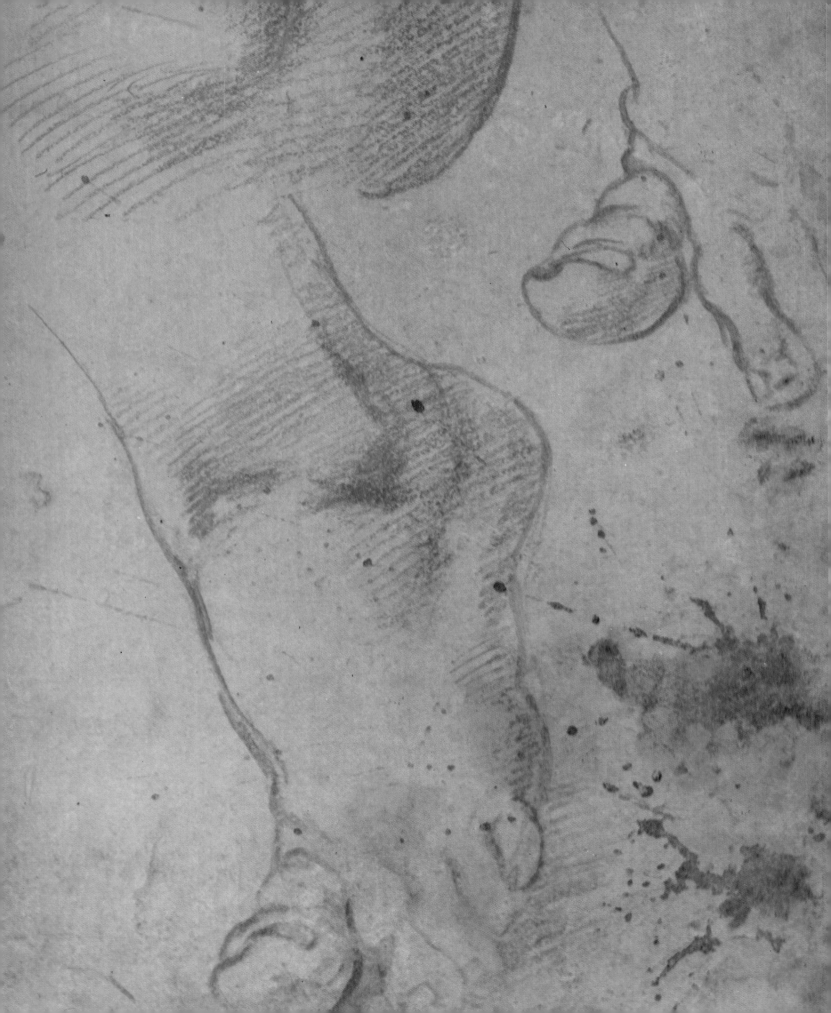

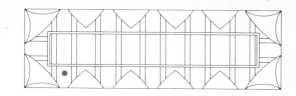

The scheme that Michelangelo finally arrived at was infinitely more ambitious than the first, so much so that he probably sought the advice of Vatican scholars. In place of the twelve apostles along the lower part of the ceiling, he alternated figures of Old Testament prophets and figures of sibyls, prophetesses from Greco-Roman mythology who also predicted the coming of a Messiah. The magnificent drawing at right, executed in reddish chalk, is a study for the Libyan sibyl, in Greek myth the daughter of Zeus and a sorceress. Michelangelo apparently first limned the finely shaded torso, whose outstretched arms hold up a massive book of prophecies in the finished fresco. On the rest of the sheet, the master carefully analyzed and rehearsed details of the figure. Beneath the torso he drew an arched foot (opposite, in detail): then, as if viewing the foot under a lens, he redid it twice, the second time focusing entirely on the great toe which bears most of the body's weight. A study of the left hand is at lower center in the drawing at right, and next to it Michelangelo repeated the face, starting to transform its features into the Hellenic beauty on the ceiling.

OVERLEAF: This detail from the Libyan sibyl study displays Michelangelo's virtuosity at rendering anatomy; it also reveals that, as with others of his female figures, he drew from a male model—a Renaissance convention. For the frescoes he softened the heavy muscles, but the figures often retain a stolid, powerful form whose sex is indeterminate.

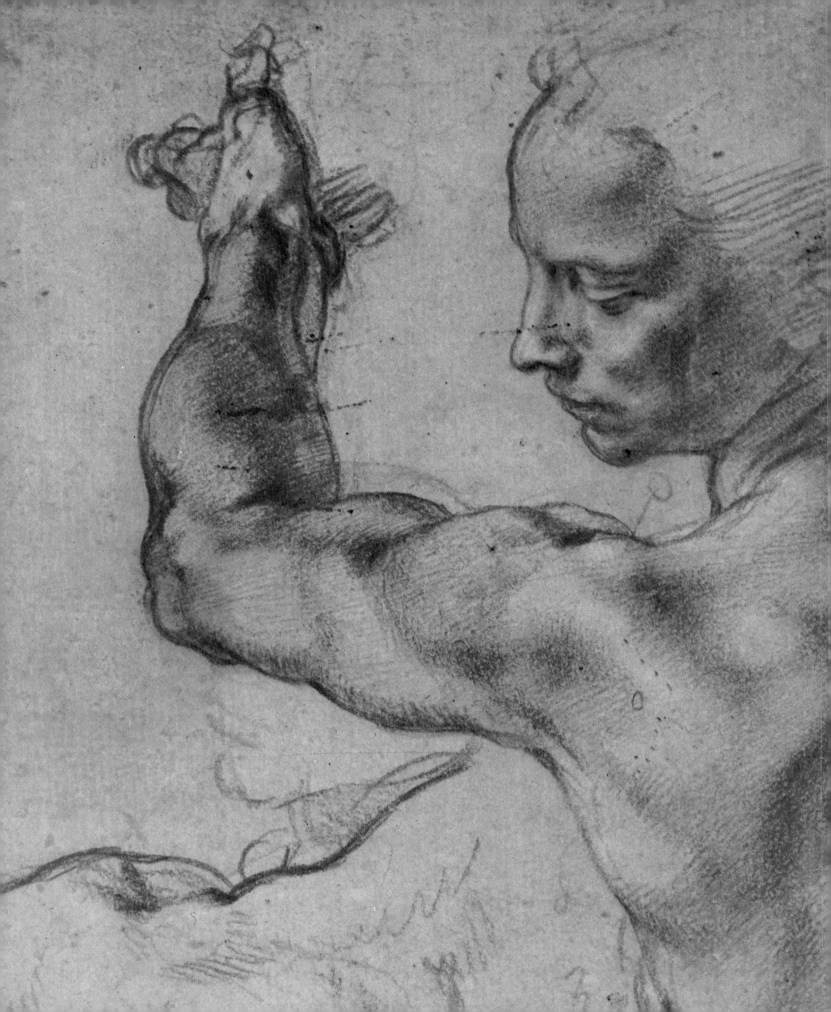

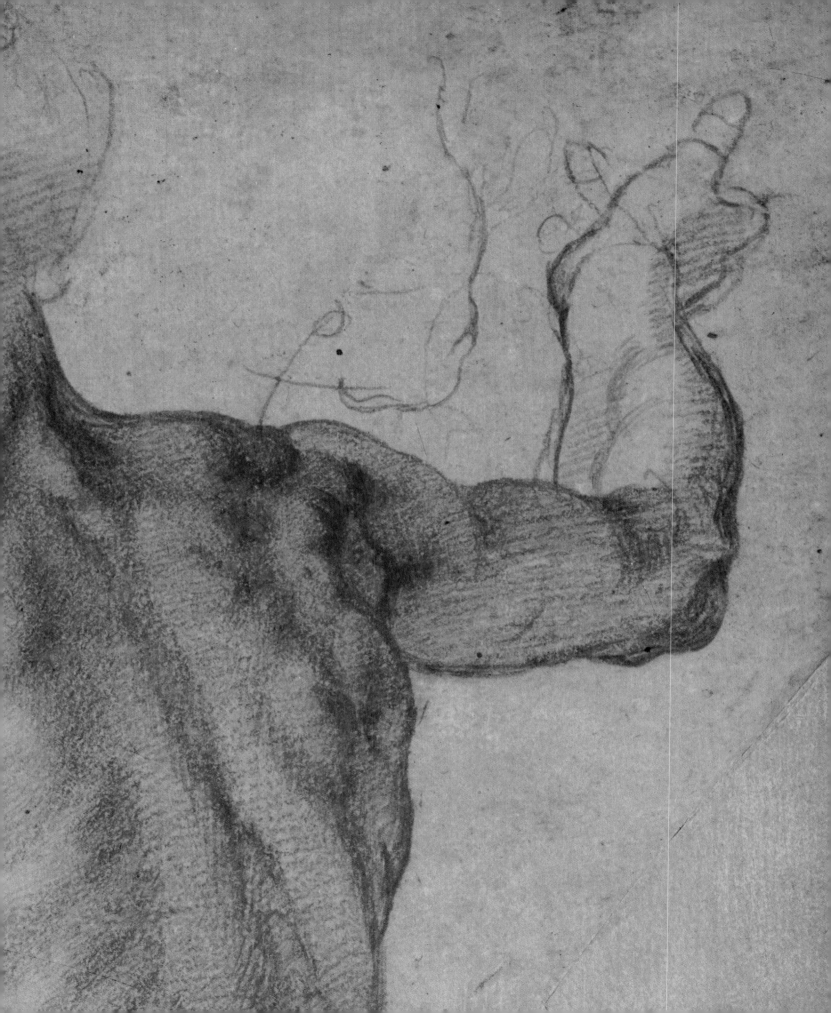

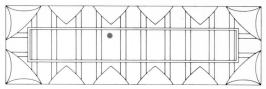

The grandeur and sheer force of Michelangelo's creativity is everywhere present in a study for his most famous image, The Creation of Adam. Here, as on the ceiling, the figure reclines in a languorous pose of extraordinary grace, his left arm reaching out to receive the touch of life from God. The Creation of Adam was one of nine episodes from the Book of Genesis that Michelangelo plotted down the center of the vault. There, as elsewhere on the ceiling, the medium he used was true fresco—watercolor painted into fresh, moist plaster. From a sketch he would make a cartoon or full-scale drawing of a scene. Atop his scaffold he transferred the design by holding the cartoon against the plaster and tracing its contours with a metal stylus. He then applied his colors and often boldly expanded the figures beyond his outlines until some reached a height of nearly eighteen feet. This arduous process, coupled with the strain of painting with his head thrown back, at times threatened to break the master. "I live in great toil and great weariness of body," he wrote to his brother late in 1509, "I have no friends...and don't want any, and haven't the time to eat what I need."

93

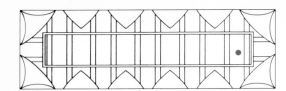

As a writer loves toying with words, or a painter with colors, Michelangelo, who remained a sculptor at heart, delighted in examining limbs and gestures from every point of view. The arms he sketched in black crayon on the sheet at right are among several dozen studies of body parts that, together, make up a sort of repertory from which the artist could freely pick. He made this particular drawing for one of his earliest scenes, which portrays Noah and his sons after the Deluge, and the spare, sure lines reflect his striving to give figures the clarity necessary for viewing them from the floor more than twenty yards below. The hand of the upper arm is also akin to that of God's in The Creation of Adam, one of the many instances where Michelangelo repeated virtually the same limb or back or torso in widely separated parts of the ceiling.

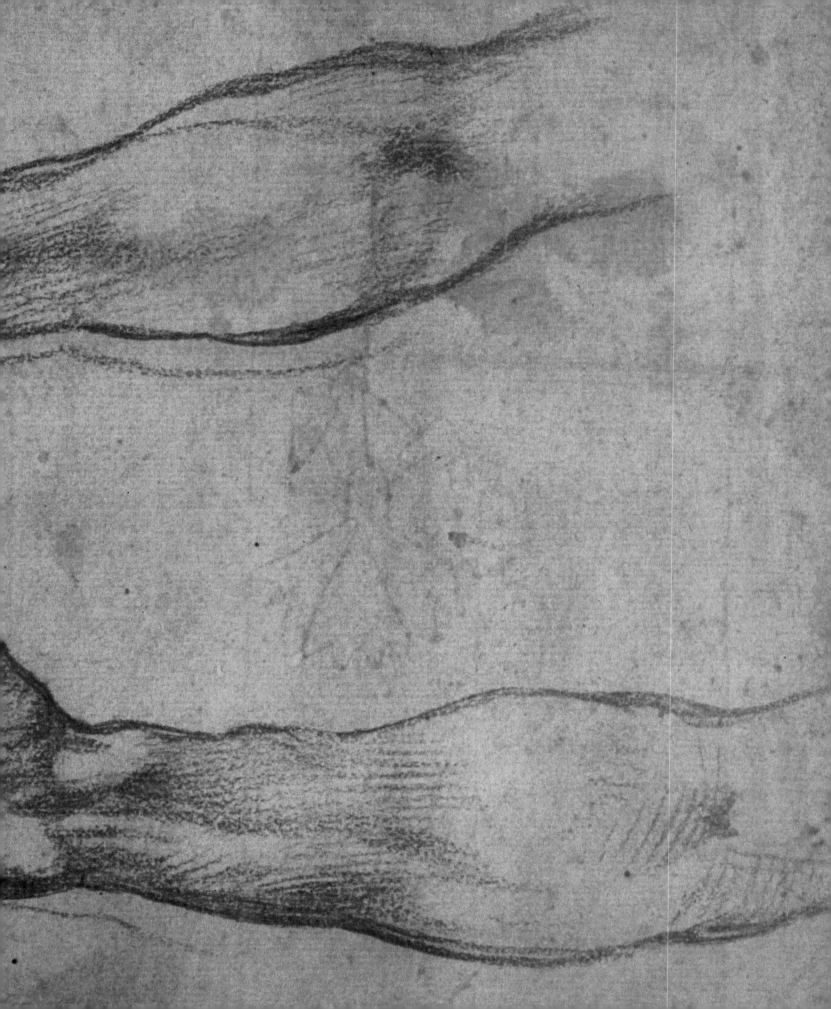

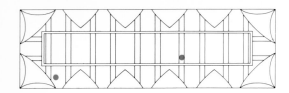

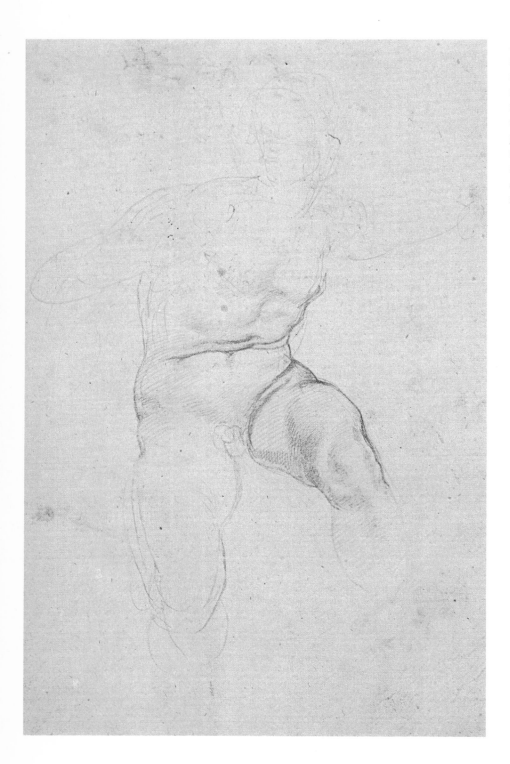

Again and again the artist turned to studies of nudes in his unceasing effort to represent physical perfection. The torso at left is for an ignudo that is above the prophet Isaiah. Like other Renaissance humanists Michelangelo greatly admired the art of classical Greece and sought to emulate the idealized beauty preserved in recovered statues. Yet he went beyond these ancient models, evoking not only sublime grace in his figures, but also the turmoil of his own personality—that of a most sensual man longing for a spiritual existence.

On the sheet opposite, Michelangelo is busily occupied with three projects. The partial nude, upper right, its fist heroically clenched, appears in fresco as a child on the left hand of the Libyan sibyl. To the left he sketched the same sibyl's right hand, replete with tendons straining from the enormous book she clasps. He covered the bottom of the sheet with six nude, bound slaves, figures that he planned as adornments for Julius's tomb. The architectural cornice, upper left, was also probably for the papal tomb, a project that Michelangelo may have worked on in 1510 before returning to complete the ceiling.

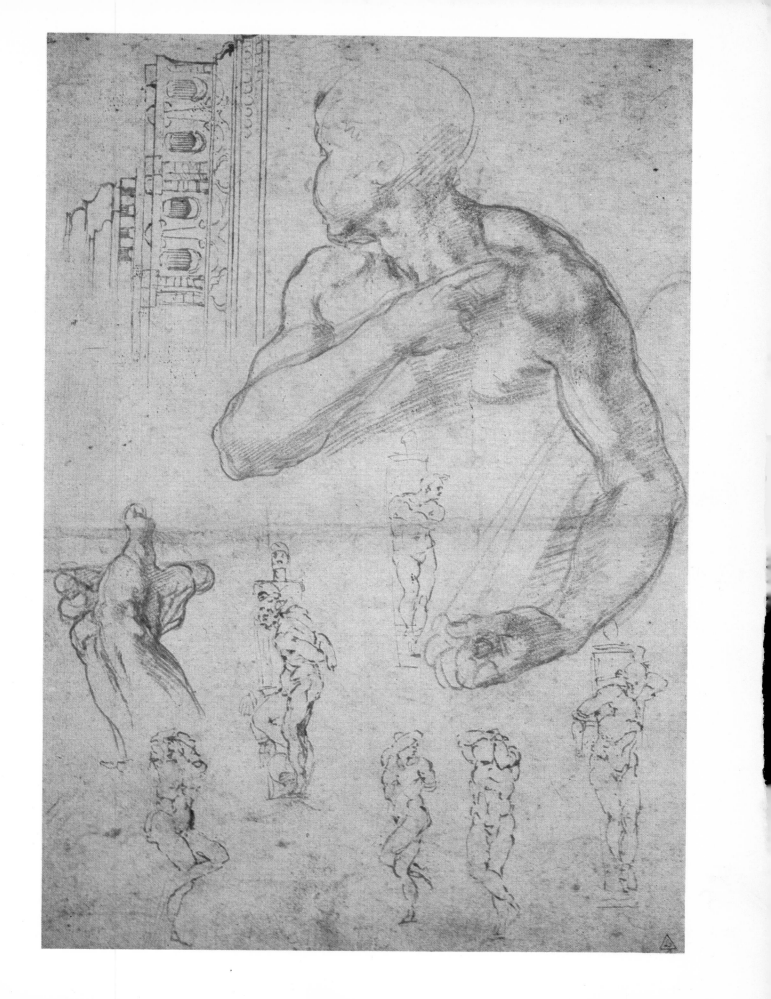

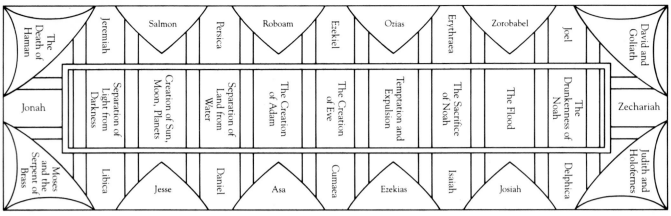

As the key above reveals, Michelangelo peopled his ceiling with Roman sibyls, Old Testament prophets, and Hebrew patriarchs, whom he united visually and thematically into a vast overture to the coming of Christ.

Michelangelo toiled at his creation, virtually unaided, for almost four years. In his quest for perfection, he would have labored even longer were it not for the impatience of Julius II, who constantly demanded to know when the artist would finish. "When I can, Holy Father," Michelangelo typically responded, until the angry pontiff struck him with his staff and later threatened to have him thrown down from the scaffold. Under such prodding Michelangelo hurried to finish, and on October 31, 1512—All Saints' Day—he at last unveiled his work.

That morning the pope celebrated Mass, as all the artists and high officials of Rome gathered inside the Sistine Chapel to gaze upon what Michelangelo had done. What they saw looked less like a painted vault than another world, populated by more than three hundred figures, many of them three and four times life-size and expressing, in their faces and bearing, extremes of anguish and ecstasy. Only the coloration, a rich harmony of naturalistic tones, was subdued. Compared to the restrained frescoes done for Sixtus IV, the ceiling was like a whirlwind, a battle of Titans—which was exactly what the tempestuous Julius liked about it.

Lending power to the imagery was the story it unfolded: the prehistory of Christianity, foretelling the New Testament. Michelangelo divided this theme, and the ceiling, into four components (diagramed above). The Genesis episodes, which he abbreviated to fit into the vault, tell of the Creation and Fall of man and his reemergence in the person of Noah, still yoked with sin and awaiting redemption. Flank-ing these events are the huge enthroned prophets and sibyls, wise beings bursting with the knowledge of what is to come. Inside the triangular compartments above the windows, Michelangelo visualized the ancestors of Christ, who link the Savior to the Old Testament Hebrews. Finally, tied to these figures are four scenes of salvation from the Old Testament that fill the corners of the vault.

As Julius wanted, the frescoes unify the chapel, connecting the ceiling to the walls below, which show Moses and the life of Christ on earth. They also invoke the authority of the pope himself. The aged prophet Zechariah, who foretold Christ's entry into Jerusalem, sits above the chapel entrance, calling attention to the pope's role as Christ's earthly vicar. And above the altar loom the Creation scenes, which not only conjure up the coming of Christ, but are the only scenes that contain portrayals of God—a bearded patriarch whose robust image must have delighted Julius. Michelangelo also made an explicit reference to his patron by encircling some of the ignudi with acorns: Rovere, Julius's family name, means "oak" in Italian.

Only four months after the chapel opened, the pope, whom Michelangelo reported was "very much pleased," died at nearly seventy years of age. Because of his ambition the city of Rome by then possessed a grandeur commensurate with the papacy. Michelangelo, now acclaimed as the Divine One, would continue to add to the papal monuments. But never again would an artist and his patron create a work that compared to the spectacle on the ceiling.

FOLDOUT→

The draftsmanship in this rendering of a youth's head is matchless, with the features drawn in chalk, then picked out in brown ink. Michelangelo may have used the study, inverting its position, as the model for the noble head of Adam.

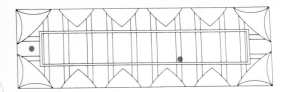

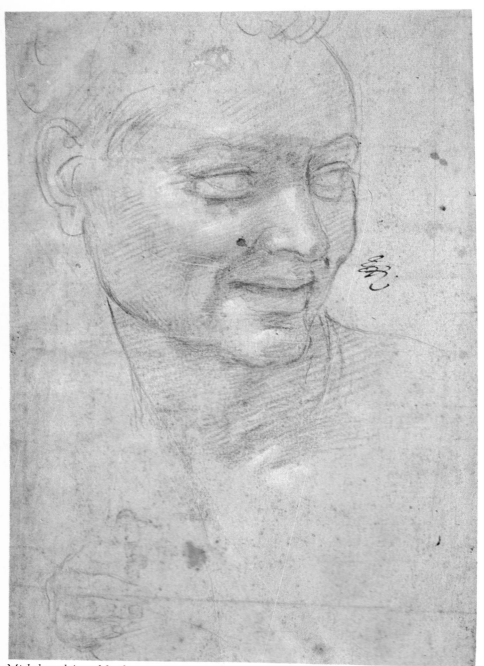

Michelangelo's zeal for drawing from live models is nowhere more evident than in this portrait of a laughing boy. His face, in fresco, appears with the nude sketched on page 96.

The upturned head opposite, and disquieting gaze, corres Jonah, who sits over the alt God springing out of the ch entrance, Jonah heralds th parable of his emerging st the resurrection, a parthe represented by the popse figure that Michelanghe arranged and painte By order of their chular Drunkenness ohe a doing so he ward by Renaissance dry, of journey from rich-Noah, to the istine course, it is amp, " ness and uh casts ceiling su " as his fr abroad

IV

URBAN VIII

ROME TRIUMPHANT

If the pope's task on earth is partly to act as impresario, then in that sense alone Urban VIII must rank with the greatest popes. Maffeo Barberini began well in the world, the son of a rich and well-connected Florentine aristocrat. Beyond that he had the wit to realize early on that his ambitions lay in the Church, and he also had the skill to manage his career. With the help of his uncle, a high-placed prelate with influence at the Vatican, Maffeo advanced in the Church. At the age of thirty-three he won an appointment as papal legate to France. His official mission was to present the Church's felicitations to King Henry IV on the birth of his son, the future Louis XIII.

Handsome and accomplished, a scholar, a poet, and a lover of the arts, Barberini made important friends in France. In 1606 strong French backing helped raise him to the College of Cardinals. In 1623 the cardinals elected him pope. Aged fifty-five, in excellent health, and looking forward to a long pontificate, he chose the name Urban—no doubt foreshadowing his resolution to remake the city

In dark bronze and shining gold, Urban VIII blesses his flock from atop his tomb. Thus, about 1647, did the sculptor Gianlorenzo Bernini portray his greatest patron.

of Rome and to fill St. Peter's Basilica with all the trappings that were proper to it.

Even as he put on the papal tiara, Urban had already chosen the man who was to accomplish these miracles. For in Rome there lived a young genius, Gianlorenzo, son of a sculptor named Pietro Bernini. Gianlorenzo had been a child prodigy, carving marble like a master before he was ten, spending his boyhood years sketching ancient Roman sculpture in the Vatican collections, and finally being brought before Pope Paul V, a predecessor of Urban VIII. The Holy Father, so the story went, loaded the young Bernini with gold medals. Turning to Cardinal Barberini, who happened to be in the room, the pope remarked, "We hope that this youth will become the Michelangelo of his century."

From that time on Bernini worked mainly for the pontiffs, while the discerning cardinal—who saw very well that Bernini was the new Michelangelo—wrote admiring verses about the sculptor's work and bided his time. When Bernini carved his celebrated statue of David, Cardinal Barberini held a mirror to Bernini's face so that the sculptor could model David's adolescent features after his own. Pope Urban VIII, as soon as he was so designated, called Bernini to his presence and said, "It is your great fortune, Cavalier, to see Cardinal Maffeo Barberini pope, but our fortune is far greater in that Cavalier Bernini lives during our pontificate." Whether the pope ever uttered so Italianate a compliment does not matter. The sense of it is true. Seldom have patron and artist been so perfectly matched. Bernini, aged twenty-five, was now the prince of all Italian artists and in the service of a patron whose ambition was to adorn the vastest church in the world.

Though many popes have been brilliant, cultivated men, perhaps none actually surpassed Urban VIII in sophistication. He had spotted Bernini as the best, but he hired many other artists also, as the notion seized him. He had studied science; Galileo Galilei, who built the first telescope and discovered the planet Jupiter's four moons, was Urban's personal friend. More than that Urban was a master of the grand gesture. In 1623 the rebuilt St. Peter's was almost

CARDINAL ANTONIO BARBERINI

PRINCE TADDEO BARBERINI

Urban VIII never forgot his position as head of his family. He raised his brother Antonio and his nephews Francesco and Antonio the Younger to the cardinalate. On his nephew Taddeo he bestowed a title, a fortune, and an aristocratic bride.

CARDINAL FRANCESCO BARBERINI

CARDINAL ANTONIO BARBERINI THE YOUNGER

complete. The church lacked decor, as well as its grandiose colonnade and piazza, but the great dome created by Michelangelo was finished, as was the facade. Yet the church had never been consecrated.

In November 1626 Urban proceeded to perform the consecration in a ceremony that lasted two days and featured processionals of cardinals and ambassadors, the blessing of twelve new red mosaic crosses, and multiple artillery salutes from Castel Sant' Angelo. Finally, Urban VIII said Mass for the crowd of thousands. The pageantry was Urbanesque: it was energetic but controlled. Even as Urban consecrated the church, a massive construction project within its very walls was already under way. For on June 30 that same year Urban had told Bernini to build him a centerpiece for the church—a canopy, or baldachin, for the main altar. No one knows what instructions Urban gave his architect, but he must have asked for a monument that would dwarf every other thing in the church and even reach into the dome.

Other popes before Urban had had an aptitude for ostentation; indeed this tendency had brought the papacy dangerously close to collapse. Julius II in the previous century had thrust himself into the limelight at every chance, and he too had been obsessed with rebuilding and beautifying St. Peter's. Leo X, who followed Julius, was more flamboyant still. His contemporaries reported that just after receiving the papal crown Leo had remarked with relish, "God has given us the Papacy. Let us enjoy it." And this offspring of the great house of Medici in Florence had been quite childishly impatient to enjoy it. Determined to make the papal court the most cultured in Europe, he spent great sums to attract accomplished writers, scholars, and poets to Rome where he freely opened the treasures of the Vatican Library to them. He enthusiastically carried on the reconstruction of St. Peter's and, as Julius II before him, encouraged Raphael to continue painting in the Vatican Palace. (The difficult Michelangelo he sent to work at a safe distance in Florence.) Indeed the pope lavished money in every direction—on plays, masques, ballets, regattas, masked balls, hunting and hawking, and on banquets featuring such surprises as flocks of nightingales flying out of huge pies.

Pope Leo's expenditures had been necessarily prodigious. His annual budget often ran as high as 600,000 ducats—in an age when a man could live comfortably on 200. Soon Leo was deeply in debt to every banking house in Rome. To make up the deficit he even created new offices to sell, and many a wealthy cleric acquired a profitable position or even became a cardinal. He also authorized what amounted to the selling of indulgences. Julius II had begun this practice to support the building of St. Peter's, but now Leo carried it to extremes.

No wonder then that a rebellion was at hand. In 1510, during the pontificate of Julius II, an obscure friar from Eisleben, Germany, visited Rome. Tourist that he was, Martin Luther caught not the slightest glimpse of papal improprieties, but he already had doubts in his heart that he carried back home with him. In 1517, under Leo's reign, Luther, now living in Wittenberg, found his doubts had turned to disgust. He never—at least not at first—intended to challenge the authority of the pope, but he did believe that the traffic in indulgences was a fit subject for ecclesiastical debate. As a beginning he wrote out ninety-five theses, or statements, and quietly posted them on the door of the local church. In so doing he ignited a volcano. Thesis Thirty-seven, to take one example, read, "Any true Christian whatsoever, living or dead, participates in all the benefits of Christ and the Church; and this participation is granted to him by God without letters of indulgences." This argument went far beyond the question of indulgences. Within a month scholars in Germany, England, Holland, and Switzerland eagerly passed reprints of the theses from hand to hand.

Leo could not bring himself to admit it, but the Protestant Reformation had begun. Even though many of his successors on the papal throne were far better men than Leo, the schism grew. The situation was further complicated when an ambitious young Austrian grand duke, Charles V, who was also king of Spain and master of the Netherlands, was elected Holy Roman Emperor and occupied

When Urban took office the facade and dome of St. Peter's were complete, as above, and the obelisk from the Roman Forum already stood in the square. Urban did not live to see the mighty colonnade Bernini later built to enclose this vast space.

northern Italy. At dawn on May 6, 1527, the imperial army of Germany and Spanish troops launched their first thunderous attack on the Holy City. By the evening of the second day, eight thousand Romans lay dead, many having first suffered torture or rape. The imperial troops wrecked churches, smashed their treasures, murdered their priests. And during the course of the sixteenth century, most of northern Europe—England, the Netherlands, the Scandinavian countries, and almost all of Germany and Switzerland—left the Catholic fold forever.

Yet the sudden, devastating shock of the sack of Rome had one salutary effect: thenceforth, even in the inmost Vatican chambers, the Church itself accepted the need for reform. And gradually the ancient institution did reform itself and did recover its influence and authority, which had looked irreclaimable. The vast committee for reform known as the Council of Trent, stretching over five papacies and adjourning only in 1565, gave the leadership of the Church an opportunity to search its soul, to reestablish Catholic doctrine, and to plan a counterattack on Protestantism. England, of course, was never to be regained, but much of central Europe returned to the Church. Spain and Venice joined the papacy to fight the Ottoman Turks and finally to defeat them in 1571 at the great naval battle in the Gulf of Lepanto, off the coast of Greece. Soon thereafter France, having rocked precariously on the brink of Protestantism, came safely back to the Catholic world when Henry of Navarre casually renounced his Protestant faith in order to gain the throne of France: so that he could become Henry IV, to whose infant son Maffeo Barberini paid his respects.

And thus the papacy that passed to Urban VIII was hardly the same office that Julius II had wielded. No longer did the pope reign over the entire Christian world. Urban VIII but dimly sensed the change. He did at least take care to live the life of a priest. No personal scandal ever touched him. He loved poetry, but as pope he wrote and commissioned religious verse. He loved music, but church music, he insisted, must be sacred in nature. One of his first papal acts was to decree that clerics had to dress as such and that they must

TEXT CONTINUED ON PAGE 118

TREASURE FOR THE HIGH ALTAR

Few of the splendidly crafted objects in St. Peter's treasury can be richer in ornamentation, or in associations, than the crucifix at left and the pair of candlesticks on page 115. The crucifix and candlesticks (two of a set of six) were the gifts of two great papal families—the Barberini and the Farnese—to the main, or high, altar at St. Peter's.

Very early in Church history, a representation of Christ on the cross came to be a requisite altarpiece for every church, and in the tenth century priests began putting candlesticks on the altar as well. One pair at first sufficed, but by Urban VIII's time the number had increased to six.

St. Peter's altarpieces took many years to make, and bear the emblems of their donors. They were bitter rivals: the Farnese had been old nobility from whose ranks a pope and several cardinals had come long before the Barberini, offshoots of a Florentine merchant prince, became prominent in Rome. Cardinal Alessandro Farnese had commissioned the crucifix and pair of candlesticks, trimmed with Farnese lilies, and had given them to the church in 1582. To the crucifix Urban VIII added his family symbol, bees, and later his nephew Cardinal Francesco commissioned four new candlesticks with bees. The beauty of the pieces outlasted the old rivalries, for the objects have acquired the luster of their locality—the pope's own altar in St. Peter's.

The silver-gilt crucifix at left, almost 6 feet tall and weighing about 130 pounds, was the work of a sixteenth-century goldsmith, Antonio Gentili. The cross itself is lapis lazuli with rock crystal medallions. Farnese lilies adorn their edges, and just below the cross are Barberini bees. The detail opposite, from the center of the cross, is the head of the crucified Christ, in gilded silver.

A century of evolving taste separates these two silver-gilt candlesticks. Above at left and in detail opposite is the one Cardinal Farnese donated to St. Peter's in 1582; above at right and in detail overleaf is Cardinal Barberini's candlestick, given to the church about 1670.

The detail opposite, of the central section in the Farnese candlestick, reveals a finely sculpted figure of Moses seated between two Grecian columns and flanked by a pair of sibyls, or prophetesses. When Antonio Gentili made these figures, he had the work of Michelangelo clearly in mind.

The artist whom Cardinal Barberini commissioned to fashion his four candlesticks for St. Peter's was Carlo Spagna, a member of a famous family of Roman metalsmiths. He may have been working from Bernini drawings. But in any case he knew the work of the great sculptor, for this angel at the base of the piece is in characteristic full motion, with flowing draperies and feathery wings.

TEXT CONTINUED FROM PAGE 111

refrain from clattering around the Roman streets in carriages, or otherwise behaving as rich laymen might. In 1625, a year when thousands of pilgrims descended upon Rome, Urban labored for months to restore some semblance of decency to the city. So well did he succeed that one visiting abbot wrote, in obvious astonishment, "For my part, I saw nothing scandalous in Rome, but, on the contrary, beheld very great piety." And a Dutch pilgrim called Urban "the great key-bearer of heaven's gate."

But as Urban too clearly perceived, the papacy was still an absolute monarchy. As was the papal wont, Urban turned his relatives into cardinals. All the Barberini amassed fortunes at the expense of the Church, becoming generous patrons of the arts and discerning purchasers of great estates. If the Roman public objected to all this—and it did object—it was free to take its spite out by scratching graffiti on the Roman walls. At least one chronic malcontent, a writer named Ferranti Pallavincine, paid with his life for criticizing the Barberini life-style.

Proud Florentine that he was, Urban always looked after his own, not only his immediate family but his dominions as well. Like his predecessor Julius II, Urban wanted the papacy to be a powerful force in international affairs, and to that end he enlarged an arms factory and built an arsenal. He strengthened existing defenses, such as those at Castel Sant' Angelo. Yet in 1641, when he went to war with the duke of Parma over an insignificant piece of territory near Rome that Urban wanted to recover for the Papal States, his armies went down to defeat. During Urban's reign all Europe was immersed in the Thirty Years' War—a long, mutual slaughtering of Catholics and Protestants. But the pope maintained his neutrality, and by the time the war ended, in 1648, the great powers of Europe had come to regard the Papal States with contempt.

But the most tragic and complex episode in Urban VIII's reign was the trial and condemnation, in 1633, of Urban's old friend the astronomer Galileo, one of the most original minds of his age, or any other. Galileo was a believer in the theories that the Polish astronomer Copernicus had published in the previous century. According to

During his uncle's pontificate, Cardinal Francesco Barberini supervised the building of a new dwelling, the Palazzo Barberini, for the papal family on the Quirinal hill. Above, in the courtyard of the spectacular edifice, a tournament is underway in honor of a royal Swedish visitor to Rome in 1656.

Copernicus the earth was not the center of the universe nor even of the solar system. The earth revolved around the sun, he said, along with other planets.

The Church and indeed the entire learned community were reluctant to accept this theory, if they were not downright hostile to it. The idea was contrary to the Bible, which asserted that the sun rose and set. Even more frightening, Copernicus had dislocated the heavens. If there were no firmament, where could the heavens be? It was an altogether terrifying prospect. Urban's predecessor Paul V, the same pope who had recognized the youthful Bernini as the new Michelangelo, had in 1616 formally condemned Copernicanism, and the Holy Inquisition had pronounced it erroneous. Galileo, in particular, had been forbidden to write about it.

Having written one book that earned him the condemnation of the Inquisition, the scientist now had been silent for many years. Naturally when his powerful admirer Barberini appeared in the papal tiara, Galileo's hopes rose. Subsequently Galileo went to visit the court in Rome, and Urban treated him as an honored guest. Now surely, he reasoned, the time had come to publish a new work in defense of Copernicus, and in 1631 he did so.

But two years later, at the age of sixty-nine, Galileo was summoned to Rome to stand trial before the Holy Inquisition. Why, they demanded, had he violated the express command of the Church to write nothing defending Copernicanism? Did he believe in this heresy? The inquisitors averred that they no longer made a practice of putting septuagenarians to the torture. And yet, as he faced them, Galileo surely knew that they, not he, could make or change the rules of the court. First he tried to deny that his book was a defense of Copernican theory. This ploy failed, since it was an obvious lie, and Galileo had to recant. Urban VIII commuted Galileo's prison sentence, but he was deeply offended. For not only had Galileo defied the Church, but in the introduction to his volume he had created a character called "Simplicius," an old-fashioned simpleton who bore a resemblance to the pope. Urban's pride was wounded. Posterity has made a villain of him for turning

On November 18, 1626, amid a throng of cardinals and ambassadors, Urban VIII, with papal staff and bishop's miter, consecrated the new St. Peter's, which had been under construction for 174 years. The pope had just commissioned a new canopy for the high altar—his great gift to the basilica.

his back on Galileo and has made a hero of the astronomer who lied to save his skin.

Meanwhile, as the inquisitors questioned Galileo, Bernini and his assistants were completing the monument that was to be, along with the Sistine ceiling and St. Peter's itself, the most grandiose of papal treasures. For in that year, after seven years' labor, the baldachin at last stood in place—over the main altar of St. Peter's, over the grave of the holy apostle himself. To obtain bronze for the canopy, which stands one hundred feet high, and the four massive, twisting columns supporting it, the architect had taken the bronze beams from the Pantheon, that best-preserved of all remaining buildings of ancient Rome. *"Quod non fecerunt barbari, fecerunt barberini ('What the barbarians dared not do, the Barberini have done')"* gibed the Romans—and in this instance the pope's own physician had invented the joke. But Urban could afford to ignore it.

His architect had truly given him immortality, had made the hand and the name and the coat of arms of Urban VIII manifest for as long as St. Peter's endured. The baldachin was both a feat of engineering and a thing of unnerving beauty. Like Michelangelo's frescoes, it defies description. Writing about it in 1682, just after Bernini's death, his biographer Filippo Baldinucci was clearly struggling for words. "The eye itself at first sight is not capable of conveying it all to the imagination."

It was by no means the only commission that Bernini executed for Urban VIII nor the last that he did at St. Peter's. He built his patron's tomb, the most remarkable in the church. He built the lovely Scala Regia, the staircase connecting the basilica with the Vatican Palaces. And much later, in the service of other popes, he built the colonnade at St. Peter's—the stately forest of columns standing in mighty ellipses around the piazza—to create what is surely the most majestic public space in the world, St. Peter's Square.

Urban died in 1644, Bernini in 1680. In a triumphant burst of energy, in each case exquisitely controlled, the two of them immeasurably enriched the grandest church in the world and made a treasure that stood for all time as a sign of renewal and revival.

THE CANOPY
OF BRONZE

A cross, symbol of Christ's sufferings, tops the baldachin above St. Peter's high altar. Toward it crawl golden bees, symbols of the Barberini pope whose monument this is.

The very word is oriental and exotic: a baldachin originally was a silken canopy, borne on four poles, that sheltered a potentate as he paraded through the streets. Along with silk itself medieval Italians imported the word from Baghdad, in the east, which they called *Baldacco*. Gradually baldachin came to mean the canopy that stood over a church altar. The baldachin of St. Peter's, which shelters the holy place where only the pope himself may say Mass, is made of gilded bronze and wood, stands 100 feet tall, and weighs a staggering 186,392 pounds. Yet this monument at the very heart of the Western Church possesses all the oriental grandeur that the word carries. No caliph, no Chinese emperor would despise it. At the same time, for all its tonnage, it is light. Soaring upward toward the airy space of Michelangelo's dome, it retains the delicate, portable look of its ancient silken prototypes.

In the seven years the baldachin took to build, its creators had their share of vexations and grief. In 1623, when Maffeo Barberini rose to the papacy, the interior of St. Peter's was relatively bare—a condition he intended to remedy, for God's greater glory and his own. To accomplish the work he hired the young Gianlorenzo Bernini, acknowledged master among all the artists of Rome. In 1626 Bernini set to work on the baldachin and ran straight into trouble. To hold the bases of the four columns he had planned, he had to sink four pits, ten feet wide and fourteen deep, in the floor of the basilica, over the site of Saint Peter's tomb. Then, to the horror of the superstitious Roman public, the diggers uncovered pagan graves. Not long afterward, several Vatican officials died sudden deaths, and Urban himself took ill. Work stopped. But the pope wisely let the fuss die down and put his architect to work again, this time with the help of a scholar who kept meticulous track of any bones, Christian or pagan, that turned up.

The greatest scandal proved to be not bones but bronze; Bernini needed some ninety tons of it. With the power of the pope behind him and a fine disregard for civic disgust, he stripped the bronze girders out of the Pantheon, a classic Roman edifice then seventeen centuries old. He even took seven bronze ribs from St. Peter's dome, replacing them with lead.

But when at last, in 1633, Urban unveiled the masterpiece, public wrath evaporated. Not even Urban's enemies grumbled about Bernini's having festooned the giant tabernacle with every known Barberini emblem—bees, laurel, sunbursts, and what appears to be the birthing of a Barberini baby. Poets wrote sonnets to the baldachin. The delighted pontiff, having already doubled Bernini's salary, now gave him a bonus. The accomplishment, as he knew, was beyond price; for the artist had given consummate form not simply to unabashed Barberini pride but to the renewed energies of the Church triumphant.

St. Peter's chair and the sunburst Bernini designed to hang above it are visible through his baldachin, which marks the high altar of the church. The baldachin's four bases hold up four muscular columns that twist upward like living things. These support a wide platform, richly ornamented, which itself supports four powerful upsurging scrolls. Atop the scrolls Bernini placed a smaller platform, crowned by the symbols of the Church: an orb and a crown.

At the top of each column, nearly one hundred feet above the church floor, stands an angel in swirling robes. One hallmark of Bernini's virtuosity was that he could make bronze or marble ripple like cloth in the wind. Between the architectural scrolls that support the orb and cross, two idealized winged children frolic—one hovering precariously over the edge with the papal tiara, the other grasping Saint Peter's keys. The babies are in fact larger than a medium-size adult. Above the baldachin in a mosaic adorning the dome, Saint John composes his gospel. He is flanked by an eagle, which is his symbol.

Theatrical and sumptuous as it is, the baldachin is also an expression of the religious faith of the artist who made it and the pope who commissioned it. The detail at left is the ceiling of the canopy as the pope would see it looking directly up from the altar that only he may use. As if to force light to penetrate the thick bronze, Bernini designed a golden sunburst, at the center of which floats a dove—symbol of the Holy Spirit—descending from the heavens.

In the lower section of his columns, Bernini finished off the fluted curves. The bronze continues to twist upward, now ornamented with cherubs and trailing foliage.

The column opposite, rising into the sphere of the dome, is an example of Bernini's genius for revitalizing old forms. In the early basilica had stood four twisted columns, possibly from Solomon's temple in Jerusalem. Bernini took his inspiration from these and emphasized the torsion by gilding the fluted spirals. At the canopy's top edge, scalloped bronze draperies hang like brocade.

OVERLEAF: *Bernini's delicately cast and gilded designs at the column bases belie the great weight each column bears. Leafy clusters curl upward, and on the bottom ring two other Barberini family emblems alternate—the golden bee and the sunburst. Like any powerful seventeenth-century patron, Urban wanted his mark on whatever he commissioned, and the artist was quite willing to oblige.*

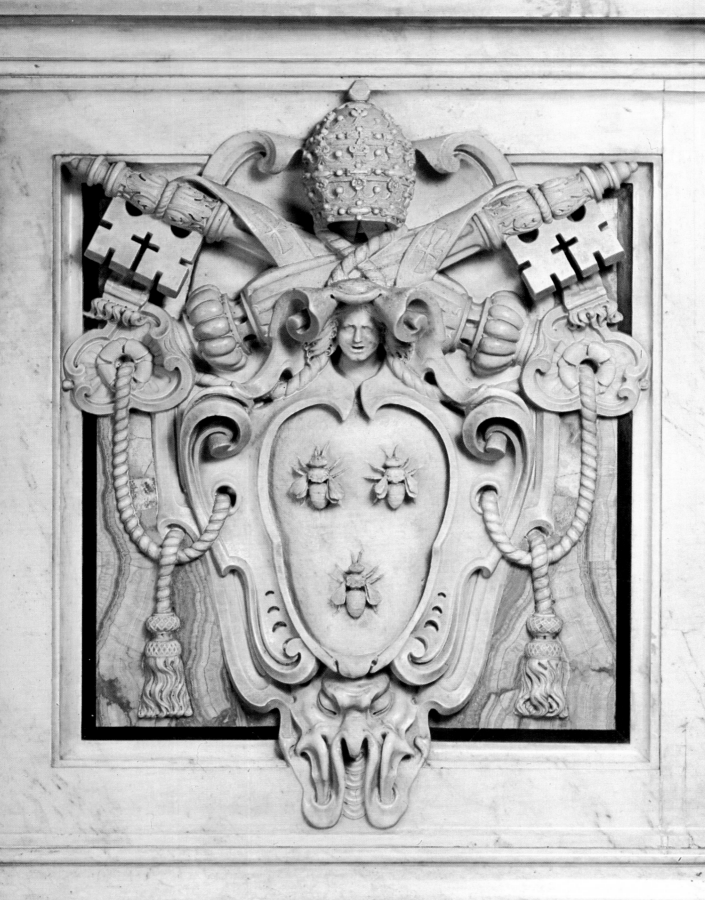

The feminine face above, calm at left, in distress at right, comes from the reliefs on the four pedestals supporting the baldachin. She is probably a Barberini princess—the pope's niece—whom Bernini portrayed in childbirth in all but one of the eight reliefs.

The four marble pedestals, or plinths, under each bronze column display the Barberini coat of arms, opposite. At the top sits the papal tiara, and below it the crossed keys of Saint Peter and a discreet portrait of Urban's niece. Tassled cords tie the keys of the Kingdom to a Barberini crest, on which the emblematic bees appear in a stately trio.

The woman giving birth contorts her features in anguish, at left, in the seventh portrait Bernini made on the marble bases of the baldachin. Her newborn son, opposite, is a husky Barberini princeling, whose head is nevertheless scarcely larger than the bees on the family crest. Urban VIII's niece, according to one story, had promised to pay for the plinths if she did, in fact, become the mother of a son. In return for her donation, she had a spectacular reward: her portrait and her son's are on the finest monument in St. Peter's—two of the few portraits within the church that are not saints, biblical figures, or popes.

V

PIUS IX

THE PAPACY LOST AND REGAINED

Thousands jammed the streets of Rome as Pius IX made his way to the papal throne on July 17, 1846, and all Europe joined in a celebration for the new "father of all the faithful," who had just granted amnesty to hundreds of political prisoners. With shouts of "Viva Pio Nono!" Italians wished long life to the pope. On that warm and cheerful day, just a month after Pius's coolly received coronation, no one—not even the most ardent reformist—could guess that the adoring crowds would turn against Pius by the end of his thirty-two-year reign, the longest and one of the most tumultuous pontificates in history.

Giovanni Maria Mastai Ferretti was a native of the Papal States, born in Senigallia in 1792 to wealthy, rather liberal parents, who encouraged their son to go into the clergy with an open, inquisitive mind. The young Ferretti had suffered epileptic attacks—one so severe that he had to discontinue his studies for a while. The attacks at length ceased, and Ferretti attributed his cure to holy water—a miraculous event that instilled in him a lifelong spirituality. As a

Pius IX, reserved and somewhat stiff in this portrait, fought a losing battle to retain the worldly powers of the Vatican during his thirty-two-year pontificate.

priest Ferretti felt the Church provided little inspiration to its congregation, and his criticisms became more severe as he moved from parish to parish. He found the institution intolerant of new ideas and inept in its dealings with governments. He worried that unless the Church paid greater heed to the popular frame of mind, it would lose influence in its proper sphere and would then be left behind—a relic of the Middle Ages.

As bishop, Ferretti attracted a large following with his leadership and his discussions of the Church's role in society. His kindness and generosity were genuine, and he ingratiated himself to all with a sharp, self-deprecating sense of humor. When a nun asked Pius to autograph a barely recognizable photograph of himself, his inscription echoed Christ's words as He walked upon the water: "Fear not, it is I!" His extraordinary good looks, melodic voice, and gentle countenance charmed even those who feared him too liberal—excluding, of course, the conservative cardinals who opposed his election to the papacy.

When Ferretti emerged from the conclave of 1846 as Pope Pius IX, his first official proclamation was a general amnesty for political prisoners in the Papal States. Ferretti had taken the name Pius in deference to Pius VII, who, thirty-two years earlier, had triumphed over the indignities he suffered at the hands of Napoleon Bonaparte. The French emperor had declared the papacy an "obsolete machine," then in 1809 had swept into Rome and occupied the Papal States. Pius VII himself he deported to France as a political prisoner. But after Napoleon's abdication in 1814, Pius returned to his beloved Rome and took possession of the papal dominions once more. Pius VII's successors had no interest in dismantling the Papal States either, or in turning over the clergy's power to the civilians.

Gregory XVI, elected in 1831, relished his absolute power and greatly reinforced the papal army. Of the European ambassadors in Rome, only the Austrians urged Gregory not to sacrifice even a fragment of his separate domain in Italy; willing to fight for its own Italian provinces, Austria even gave military and economic aid to the Papal States. But the people of Italy would not give up, and had

An assassin lunges for Pius's prime minister Pellegrino Rossi, above. The pope had many enemies—chiefly European reformers bent on abolishing the Vatican's political power—and his resistance cost him dearly. Rossi's murder brought the Papal States one step closer to extinction.

Pius IX not succeeded Gregory, the Papal States might have exploded then in a blaze of revolution.

Pius's acts of reform made him the champion of the people. In addition to amnesty, he ordered the return of exiles, rewrote unjust laws, reorganized the judiciary and penal codes, made important changes in financial administration, and restructured the powerful council of ministers into a civilian body. He encouraged new developments in agriculture and science. He established a free press, and scores of newspapers and journals began to appear. By the summer of 1847—after just one year on the throne—Pius had aligned the papacy with liberal Europe.

Realizing that the presence of Austrian troops in Italy unnerved the reformists and made his office seem dependent on foreign support, Pius discouraged further foreign intervention. Prince Metternich of Austria, the aging diplomat who was the sworn enemy of everything radical, bitterly declared, "We were prepared for anything but a liberal pope."

Whenever Pius passed through the streets and squares of Rome, he was disturbed by enthusiastic cries from citizens cheering him on. Though he was glad to have won popular support for the papacy, he was certainly not prepared to declare war on Austria, which is exactly what his flock was calling for. Although he could understand why some people might want such a war, he could not conceive of a holy man as the general of an army, nor of members of his Church fighting one another. While Europe rushed inexorably toward the revolutions that were soon to engulf it, the pope—whose cautious reforms were now dismissed as unworthy of their time—was swept aside in the general flood. Metternich predicted that Pius's hesitancy would cost him his sovereignty. "Each day the pope shows himself more and more lacking in common sense," wrote the prince. "Born and brought up in a liberal family, he has been formed in a bad school; a good priest, he has never turned his mind toward matters of government...if matters follow their natural course, he will be driven out of Rome."

As Pius backtracked and tried to dissociate his popular reforms from the issue of Italian unity, he looked like a reactionary hostile to the national cause. People turned against him, and crowds taunted the highest clergy members. In desperation Pius appointed moderate laymen to political offices, thinking that such measures would appease his enemies. But after his prime minister Pellegrino Rossi had declared that the papacy was "the one great thing left to Italy," a mob went after Rossi and killed him. The day after the assassination, armed gangs sang praises to the "heroic" murderers and gathered at the Piazza del Popolo to shout for the end of the pope's government. Declaring that if he gave way he would henceforth be allowed only "to pray and to bless," the pope at first stood his ground. But as a field gun was brought up into the piazza and bullets smashed through windows of the papal palace on the Quirinal hill, Pius was pressed to surrender. And when civilians at last set up a radical government, the pope saw that nothing, not even his office, was sacred. After just over two years on the throne, Pius had to flee Rome.

But Europe took pity on the pope. Even those who had no stake in the outcome of his struggles offered him comfortable, safe retreat. Queen Victoria invited the pope to stay in England. Pius finally chose Gaeta in the kingdom of Naples, south of the Papal States, and laid plans to escape with the help of French and Bavarian ambassadors. The French ambassador would call upon the pope as if on official business. While the Frenchman read dispatches in a loud voice, the pontiff would disguise himself as an ordinary priest and slip out to a waiting carriage—as the accomplice ambassador read on.

The pope arrived safely at the church where the Bavarian ambassador was waiting to drive him out of the city through the Lateran gate and up into the Alban Hills. Here the ambassador's wife was waiting in a carriage. Pius climbed in beside her, carrying the same ciborium, or sacramental vessel, that Pius VI had used while a prisoner in France before his death in 1799. Once safe at Gaeta, the pope announced that he had left his capital and had sought refuge outside the Papal States, "so as not to compromise my dignity or appear to approve of the excesses that...might take place in Rome."

In 1850 Louis Napoleon, president of France and soon to be

On shaky political ground Pius IX, on the portico (at right, above) of the church of San Giussepe dei Falegnami, preaches to a crowd among the ruins of the Roman Forum. French troops on loan to the Vatican ring the congregation to discourage rioters and would-be assassins.

Emperor Napoleon III, came to Pius's rescue and with thousands of soldiers restored the pope to his former office in Rome. The emperor's motive was of course selfish, since a politically fragmented Italy with a powerful papacy vying for control with the civil government would be no threat to the security of France. Bayonet-carrying Frenchmen swarmed around the Vatican.

But the Papal States had already begun their ultimate decline. Pius IX's negligible army, even with French reinforcements, could not hope to stave off the unification of the Italian state. Radicals, liberals, and conservatives allied in aid of that cause. Such men as Giuseppe Mazzini, the radical leader, wanted a united republic. The soldier Giuseppe Garibaldi, together with the ruling house of Sardinia, wanted to establish a united kingdom. In either case papal sovereignty would be at an end.

Barred from the political realm and stripped of his worldly powers, Pius turned his attention to spiritual matters. He had returned from exile an embattled man and an enemy of all attempts to modernize the Church. Pius refused to have anything to do with Italian unification and, from his tiny sovereign state, did all he could to keep what he regarded as irreligious ideas out of the Church. He considered what was happening in Italy a revolt against decency and morality. And he was determined to see the Catholic faith renewed. In 1854 Pius had put forth the dogma of the Immaculate Conception and thus caused a new flowering of devotion to the Mother of Christ.

He also sought to squelch political liberalism within Church ranks. One of the most pointed of his measures was the Syllabus of Errors, a formal rejection of social change, biblical criticism, and the separation of Church and state. The syllabus lists eighty "principal errors of our time," which leave no doubt about the Church's position: the eightieth error is the view that "the Roman pontiff can or should reconcile himself to and agree with progress, liberalism, and modern civilization."

In 1869 Pius summoned the First Vatican Council and steered its more than seven hundred delegate bishops toward adopting his definition of papal infallibility. The Council did pass this controver-

In December 1869, Pius IX, rising from his throne in this print, opened the First Vatican Council to more than seven hundred bishops from around the world. At Pius's urging the council declared the pope infallible in matters of Catholic faith and morals.

sial doctrine—its point is the pope's teaching authority in matters of faith and morality—and its effect was to support Pius's stand against modern rationalism and liberalism.

For twenty years after his return from Gaeta, the pope held his ground in Rome, even after Victor Emmanuel II, the erstwhile king of Sardinia, was crowned as the first king of Italy in 1861. But the alliance with France fell apart. In 1870 the Prussians attacked Napoleon III, and as the French armies prepared to depart, Italian militants prepared to attack.

Pius had almost no means of retaliation. To the pontiff the Italian soldiers were thieves, monsters of hell, children of Satan. Yet he prepared to resist. He drove to St. John Lateran, drew up the small papal army for review, and on his knees ascended the Scala Sancta— the stairs that Christ is said to have climbed in Pontius Pilate's palace in Jerusalem and that had been brought to Rome in the fourth century. At the summit Pius prayed, then stood up. But rather than sending his soldiers to war, he blessed them—the last official act of a pope in papal Rome, on September 19, 1870. Within hours the troops began their bombardment of the city gates, and Pius raised the white flag on the cupola of St. Peter's. Rome was now irrevocably a part of the united kingdom of Italy. Pius IX withdrew into the Vatican as a "voluntary prisoner," repudiating the terms offered him. When he received his first annual payment of 3,225,000 lire for his lost territories, he declined to accept the settlement. "I need money badly," he confessed. "But what do you bring me? Just a part of what you stole from me. . . . I will never take it."

But in spite of his humiliation and defeat, the pope won a kind of victory. In declining to bend to the winds of prevailing thought in the modern world, Pius won the respect and loyalty of those Roman Catholics whose views of his pontificate were expressed by one cardinal: "When the history of the pontificate of Pius IX shall be written, it will be found to be one of the most resplendent, majestic, and powerful—one that has reached over the whole extent of the Church with greater power than that of any other pope in the whole succession." But even those who did not share this view could not deny the dignity and effectiveness of Pio Nono's last years when he saved the Holy See from bankruptcy.

Without his government Pius had no revenues, but from his isolation in the Vatican he saved the Church by reviving the medieval taxes and donations known as Peter's pence. This meant, simply, that he solicited contributions from his flock. Spreading the word throughout the Catholic hierarchy, Pius had bishops and priests appealing to the world's growing number of churches for contributions on his behalf. And the gifts came from Catholics all over the world. Treasures arrived from international leaders, too; whether or not Christian or even sympathetic to the Papal States, the most powerful presidents, kings, and queens gave gold, silver, and precious jewels in deference to Pius's holy office. And with this wealth Pius restored the papal treasury. Many of the gifts were sacred objects used in Mass, Benediction, and other services, and the individual pieces were inscribed to Pius and dedicated to either the Virgin Mary or Saint Peter, to whom the pope looked both for his authority and his inspiration.

Pius managed to emerge as a strong force in Italy, despite his political downfall, and even as he promulgated extreme—indeed reactionary—views. He dispatched missionaries to more countries than any of his predecessors had and welcomed the Catholic congregations springing up in Canada, Australia, and the United States, as well as those revitalized throughout Europe. To these millions of faithful Pius was a saint—a man to be revered for his long tenure and admired for his survival.

Pius had not merely ignored the social and political changes around him; he had actively tried to combat them with religious doctrines. By encouraging devotion to Saint Peter, Pius declared himself an heir to the powers of the first disciple of Christ and the origins of supreme papal authority. The dogma of the Immaculate Conception, which gave rise to the renewed veneration of the Virgin Mary, had enhanced Pius's position as a spiritual leader. As harsh as some of his tenets were, particularly the punitive Syllabus of Errors, Pius was most of all a paternal figure to his flock, for whom he had

Pius IX stands on the platform of his personal railroad car, on which he traveled throughout Italy to make speeches about the doctrines he hoped would revive the spiritual authority of the Vatican. One of these doctrines was his renewal of the cult of the Virgin Mary and another was a plan for donations to the papacy called Peter's pence.

delivered the Church from the ravages of the modern world.

In Rome Pius had always been active in the development of social institutions and in restoring ancient buildings of the city, particularly its churches and public squares. He ordered major reconstruction or embellishment of many venerable Roman basilicas—Santa Maria Maggiore, San Lorenzo Fuori Le Mure, and San Paolo Fuori Le Mure among them—and commissioned statues of Saint Peter and Saint Paul. In 1852 Pius began one of the most important collections of early Christian art by arranging the permanent exhibition of objects found in the catacombs. Had Pius not had to rescue the Church's finances, he would no doubt have been more of a patron of the arts, for he loved the tradition of sculpture and painting within the Church and showed himself to be a connoisseur of the finest materials and craftsmanship.

Up to the moment he died, in 1878, Pius was a controversial figure. Even in 1881, to the horror of the devout, a mob hurled stones at the pope's coffin as it was being moved for final burial. Pius was not the only pope to die a self-styled prisoner in the Vatican. Until 1929 all his successors were thus confined. But finally a concordat between Church and state established the Vatican City State as an entity independent of Italy.

Though Pope Pius IX was the last pontiff to rule as head of a sovereign state, the papacy has continued to exert a palpable authority over matters both temporal and spiritual. At least one reason for the Church's longevity is that its spiritual force is manifest in a thousand material objects, of whatever degree of magnitude. From the dozens of liturgical treasures that poured into the Vatican to comfort and aid Pope Pius to the imposing bronze baldachin over the high altar of St. Peter's, from the frescoes on the Sistine ceiling to a faded wall painting in the catacombs of a shepherd carrying his lamb, papal treasures have served one purpose and have somehow united in one artistic whole. The treasures of the papacy, all together, are the emblems of an institution that has prevailed. They are the symbols of an office that has struggled to dwell, with equal commitment, in both the material and spiritual worlds.

TRIBUTE TO
A POPE

A topaz occupies the center of this clasp of crystals, an aquamarine, and a garnet. It is one of scores of gifts the faithful showered on the papacy in the nineteenth century.

Having turned his attention from worldly politics to spiritual matters late in his reign, Pius IX was immediately rewarded by the Church faithful who inundated him with gifts—reaffirming his religious authority and refilling the Church's nearly empty treasury with golden swords, jeweled crowns, and cups of gold and silver. The tiaras, chalices, vestments, and altarpieces on the following pages have been used since their donation in the central ritual of the Church: the celebration of the Mass.

Pius's tastes in ecclesiastical objects became as old-fashioned as his politics, and the gifts he most cherished reflected his passion for splendid materials and design. He forsook simple vestments for elaborately brocaded ones, and many of his garments and ceremonial regalia were encrusted with enormous jewels. If the pope happened not to like a gift, he either hid it away, sold it, or had it altered to his liking: unhappy with a solid gold harness from Turkey, Pius had a goldsmith recast it into the diamond-studded chalice on page 157.

The treasures of the pope restored not only wealth to the Vatican but majesty as well, and the gifts that arrived at Pius's door—overdone or embarrassingly grandiose as some of them indisputably were—brought back to the papacy an appearance of former power and of ancient authority.

A dove, the Christian symbol of peace and purity, flutters on the golden hilt (left) of Pius IX's spadone, or sword, a ceremonial weapon of saintly martyrdom. The sword, its forty-five-inch blade gilded and inscribed with the pontiff's name, holds four female figures, which represent the virtues of strength, faith, justice, and charity.

The tiara opposite, a stack of three crowns representing the Holy Trinity, is, like all papal headdresses, surmounted by a cross—this one of gold and diamonds atop a globe of lapis lazuli. Pius IX's coat of arms—in twin enamel medallions—is affixed to each of the two silver fillets. The pope chose the jeweled tiara, in detail on pages 148–149, for his coronation in 1846. Thus it became an emblem of the papacy's secular powers.

Lilies, expressing the purity of the Virgin Mary, fill this detail from the papal tiara presented to Pius IX in 1877. Semiprecious stones of many colors stud the flowering vine, which is separated by bands of gold trimmed with blue enamel. The flowers stand against a field of silver mesh, required as the basic material in all papal tiaras: the whiteness of the precious metal symbolizes purity and chastity.

Woven of pure gold and silver, this rich vestment is
called the Fiddleback Chasuble for the panels of
fabric embroidered with fiddleback ferns, which, because their beauty is hidden in the thick of forests,
symbolize Christian humility. Radiant emblems of
the Holy Ghost and Saint Peter are also embroidered
into the chasuble—a sleeveless ritual vestment—the
back of which is shown above. At left, in a detail of
the chasuble's front side, the Virgin Mary wears a
halo of diamonds and stands on an image of eternity,
a red-eyed snake biting its tail. Pius IX received the
vestment in 1867 from the citizens of Bergamo, a
town in northern Italy.

The silver lectern and illuminated missal at left, gifts to Pius IX from the directors of the seven major hospitals of Rome, celebrate the fiftieth anniversary of his ordination; the lectern is inscribed in Latin with the date April 18, 1869, ". . . on which day fifty years from here Pius IX first said Mass." The leather-bound liturgical book is appropriately open to the Canon, the central part of the Mass. The lectern is decorated with gilded figures of the apostles, gilt and enamel flourishes, and a jewel-haloed Virgin Mary encircled by rhinestones.

Pius IX used the chalice at left—a silver-gilt cup atop a jeweled, enameled stem and pedestal—in a special Mass in 1875. In the detail of the chalice, opposite, a gilt paten, or plate, rests atop the cup. The surface of the paten is enameled with a lamb, the enduring symbol of Christ, whose Body and Blood are represented by the bread and wine at Holy Communion. A ninth-century papal decree required that the consecrated vessels of the Eucharist—once humbly fashioned from wood, glass, and horn—be made only with precious metals.

POLISH CHALICE

PEARL AND GARNET CHALICE

These chalices of gold and silver were favorites of Pius IX, who used them in special Masses. The one opposite on the left, presented by the Catholics of Leopolis, Poland, to Pius in 1869 on the fiftieth anniversary of his ordination as bishop, bears reliefs and figurines of angels and of Polish saints. Pearls and garnets stud the gilded silver chalice opposite on the right, the pearls looping the scalloped pedestal as if in strands. Five hundred diamonds and red and blue enamel encrust the golden wine cup at right and in detail overleaf, which Pius ordered made from a fancy harness he received from the sultan of Turkey. The pope first used the diamond chalice in 1854.

CHALICE WITH DIAMONDS

OVERLEAF: A braid of enamel, dotted with diamonds, encircles the base of the chalice above. The goldsmith who created the cup from a harness first melted down the metal, then inlaid it with enamel. Pius IX chose this chalice over all others for Masses during Christmas and Easter —as have all his successors.

Three angels, one in detail opposite, pray at the base of the monstrance at right, a vessel for displaying the Host, the wafer consumed as Christ's Body in Mass. Church law required that the Host, which would be visible through the windowpane, rest in a gilded holder and not touch the glass. A topaz-filled cross surmounts the silver and gilt sculpture, which includes busts of the four evangelists, Matthew, Mark, Luke, and John, as well as a pelican, a sacred ancient symbol of Christ. The people of Besançon France, gave the monstrance to Pius in 1850.

OVERLEAF: *Piercing its chest with its bill, the pelican from the monstrance above sheds its own blood, as Christ sacrificed himself for his flock. Topazes and garnets frame the glass circle.*

The monstrance at left, and in detail opposite and on pages 166-167, also made of gilded silver, is a rare form of tribute to the Virgin Mary, whose figure rides on clouds beneath the great star of gold. Three of the archangels—Michael, Raphael, and Gabriel—occupy the shrine beneath the Virgin, who holds a sword to smite evil. Precious jewels and variously colored stones are set in the monstrance.

Six angels, each kneeling on a jeweled pedestal, pray to the Virgin Mary, who stands above them—a position in keeping with the heavenly hierarchy. A Parisian goldsmith cast the angels in silver and gilded them before affixing the individual sculptures to the monstrance.

OVERLEAF: *A sunburst of gold radiates from the gilded cradle meant to house the Host, which is the central object of adoration in the Church.*

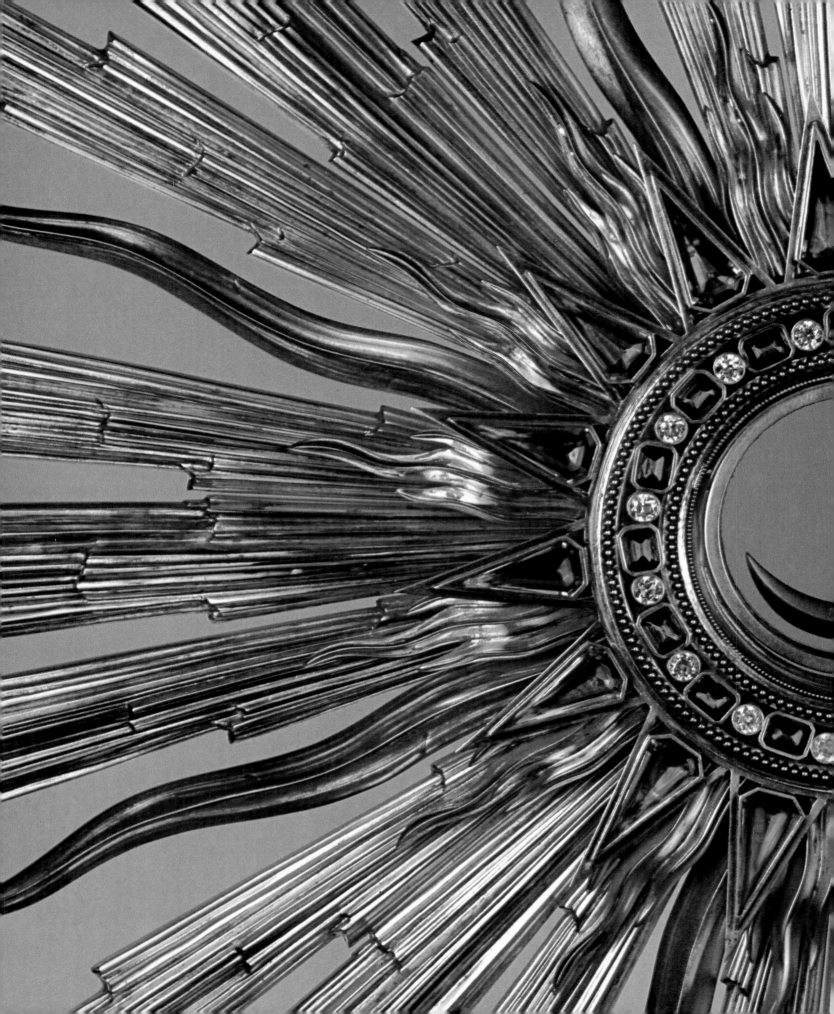

THE POPES: A CHRONOLOGY

POPES	EVENTS	ART AND ARCHITECTURE
	EARLY AND MEDIEVAL	
48-64 PETER	64 Rome burns; Emperor Nero begins first persecutions of Christians; Peter martyred	c. 200 First catacomb paintings
	c. 200 Christians use catacombs as tombs	c. 300 Sancta Sanctorum in the old Papal Palace of the Lateran first used to keep the most venerated treasures of the Church
	258 Saint Lawrence martyred for refusing to relinquish Church's treasures	
314-335 SYLVESTER I	303 Diocletian persecutes Christians	
	313 Constantine the Great champions Christianity	c. 330 Old St. Peter's constructed
	330 Constantinople is capital of Roman Empire	
	337 Death of Constantine	
	410 Goths invade Italy	
440-461 LEO I	452 Huns invade Italy	
	455 Vandals invade Italy	
	468 Lombards invade Italy	529 Foundation of Saint Benedict's monastery built at Monte Cassino; monastic buildings begin to appear
590-604 GREGORY I	c. 600 Monks go out as missionaries to western Europe and England	
752 STEPHEN II	752 Stephen makes alliance with Pepin the Short, gaining land that became the Papal States	
795-816 LEO III	800 Leo crowns Charlemagne Holy Roman Emperor, and the Church prospers under him	
817-824 PASCHAL I	846 Saracens from Arabia invade Rome, pillage St. Peter's	
1073-1085 GREGORY VII		c. 1145 Building of Vatican Palace begins
1294-1303 BONIFACE VIII	1305 Clement relocates the papacy in Avignon	
1305-1314 CLEMENT V		
1370-1378 GREGORY XI	1378 Papacy returns to Rome, to reside in the Vatican	
1378-1389 URBAN VI	1378-1417 The Great Schism divides the Church	
1417-1431 MARTIN V	1414-1417 Council of Constance ends the Great Schism	
1447-1455 NICHOLAS V	1440 Frederick III becomes Holy Roman Emperor	
	RENAISSANCE	
1455-1458 CALIXTUS III	1453 Turks capture Constantinople	
1458-1464 PIUS II	1459 Pius calls Congress of Mantua to appeal for a crusade—ignored by Europe	1460 Pius has Bernardo Rossellino rebuild Corsignano, renamed Pienza, for the papacy
1471-1484 SIXTUS IV		1473 Sistine Chapel built
1484-1492 INNOCENT VIII		

1492-1503 ALEXANDER VI

1503-1513 JULIUS II

1492-1494 Pinturicchio paints in the Borgia apartments

1499 Cesare Borgia seizes most of Papal States for Alexander

1505 Julius orders Michelangelo to begin work on the pope's tomb in the Castel Sant' Angelo

1506 Michelangelo constructs bronze monument to Julius in Bologna
Julius orders rebuilding of St. Peter's Basilica by Bramante

1510 Martin Luther visits Rome from Germany

1510-1514 Raphael's Stanze frescoed

c. 1511 Julius, with his papal army, conquers territories for the Papal States

1512 Michelangelo finishes painting the Sistine ceiling

1514 Raphael works briefly on St. Peter's Basilica after Bramante's death

1513-1521 LEO X

1517 Martin Luther nails his Ninety-five Theses to church door; Reformation begins

1534-1549 PAUL III

1527 Emperor Charles V sacks Rome and pillages the Vatican

1545 Council of Trent undertakes the reform of the Church

1555-1559 PAUL IV

1547 Michelangelo works on St. Peter's

1585-1590 SIXTUS V

1571 Turks defeated at Gulf of Lepanto

1585 Giacoma della Porta carries out Michelangelo's scheme for St. Peter's Basilica

POST-REFORMATION

1605-1621 PAUL V

1623-1644 URBAN VIII

1626 Urban consecrates St. Peter's

1626 Bernini begins work on the baldachin for St. Peter's

1629 Bernini completes building of Palazzo Barberini

1631 Galileo publishes work in defense of Copernicanism

1633 Galileo tried and convicted of heresy

1633 Bernini unveils the baldachin

1657 Bernini builds St. Peter's Square

1663 Bernini builds the Scala Regia

1775-1799 PIUS VI

1800-1823 PIUS VII

1809 Napoleon Bonaparte takes the Papal States and deports Pius as political prisoner

1814 Napoleon abdicates; Pius returns to Rome

1831-1846 GREGORY XVI

1846-1878 PIUS IX

1846 Pius declares amnesty for political prisoners in the Papal States

1848 Pius flees Rome when civilians set up radical government

1850 Louis Napoleon sends soldiers to restore Pius to Rome

1852 Pius begins collection of early Christian art

1854 Pius puts forth the dogma of the Immaculate Conception

1861 Victor Emmanuel II is crowned first king of Italy

1864 Pius puts forth Syllabus of Errors

1867 Fiddleback Chasuble given to Pius by citizens of Bergamo, one of many treasures Pius received from donors all over the world

1869 Pius calls First Vatican Council, which adopts Pius's definition of papal infallibility

1869 Silver lectern and illuminated missal given to Pius by the directors of hospitals in Rome

1870 Prussians attack France, and Napoleon III withdraws his troops from Rome
Papal States become part of a united Italy
Pius withdraws into the Vatican as a "voluntary" prisoner

c. 1870 Pius orders major reconstruction of Roman basilicas such as Santa Maria Maggiore and San Lorenzo Fuori Le Mure

1922-1939 PIUS XI

1929 Concordat establishes the Vatican City State

ACKNOWLEDGMENTS & CREDITS

We would like to thank the following for their assistance: Dr. Robert Calkins, Cornell University, Ithaca, N.Y.; Dr. Theodore Feder, Editorial Photocolor Archives, N.Y.; Mons. Ennio Francia and Giorgio Patrignani, Capitolo di San Pietro in Vaticano; Geraldine Howard, Time Editorial Services, N.Y.; David Lees, Florence; Dott.ssa Silvia Meloni, Soprintendenza per I Beni Artistici e Storici di Firenze; Pontifical Commission for Social Communications, Città del Vaticano; Padre Alfonso Rossi, Città del Vaticano; Simonetta Toraldo, Time-Life News Service, Rome; Dott. Pietro Torrito, Soprintendente per I Beni Artistici e Storici di Siena; Ecc.za Rev. Mons. Pietro Van Lierde, Vicario Generale di Sua Santitá per la Cittá del Vaticano; Sac. Giotto Vegni, Museo del Duomo, Pienza.

Maps by H. Shaw Borst
Endsheet design by Cockerell Bindery/TALAS
Mechanical production by Barbara Kraus

Cover: Maurice Babey/Ziolo. 2: Colorphoto Hinz, Basel. 4-5: Scala/Editorial Photocolor Archives. 6: Leonard von Matt/Photo Researchers. 11: Pontificia Commissione di Archeologica Sacra, Rome. 12: John Rylands University Library of Manchester, England. 13: Scala/Editorial Photocolor Archives. 14-15: Mauro Pucciarelli, Rome. 16: Scala/Editorial Photocolor Archives. 17: Erich Lessing/Magnum. 18-19: Leonard von Matt/Photo Researchers. 20 top: Erich Lessing/Magnum. 20 bottom: Scala/Editorial Photocolor Archives. 21: Erich Lessing/Magnum. 22-23: Mauro Pucciarelli, Rome. 24: Scala/Editorial Photocolor Archives. 25: Mario Carrieri, Milan. 26-27: Edizioni Torre, Rome. 28-41: Leonard von Matt/Photo Researchers. 43-45: Scala/Editorial Photocolor Archives. 46: British Museum. 47: Scala/Editorial Photocolor Archives. 48-49: Maurice Babey/Ziolo. 50-51: Leonard von Matt/Photo Researchers. 52-53: Scala/Editorial Photocolor Archives. 54-55: Topkapi Palace Museum, Sonia Halliday, London. 56: Scala/Editorial Photocolor Archives. 57: Ernst Heiniger, Zurich. 58-61: David Lees, Florence. 62-63: Giraudon. 64-69: David Lees, Florence. 71: Mark Kaufman, Life Magazine, © Time Inc. 72-78: Scala/Editorial Photocolor Archives. 79: Lauros-Giraudon. 81: Mauro Pucciarelli, Rome. 82: Biblioteca Medicea Laurenziana, Florence. 84-85: British Museum. 86: Detroit Institute of Arts. 87: Casa Buonarotti, Florence. 88-91: Metropolitan Museum of Art, N.Y. 92-93: British Museum. 94-95: Museum Boymans-van Beunigen, Rotterdam. 96: Casa Buonarotti, Florence. 97: Ashmolean Museum, Oxford. 99-102: Photo Balestrini, Rome. 103: British Museum. 104: Louvre, Paris. 105: Casa Buonarotti, Florence. 106: Dmitri Kessel, Paris. 108-109: Biblioteca Apostolica Vaticana, Archivo Fotografico, Rome. 110-111: Photo Tomisch, Rome. 112-117: David Lees, Florence. 118-119: Mauro Pucciarelli, Rome. 120: Musei Vaticani, Archivo Fotografico, Rome. 121: Dmitri Kessel, Life Magazine, © Time Inc. 122-125: Scala/Editorial Photocolor Archives. 126-127: Ron Weidenhoeft/Saskia/Editorial Photocolor Archives. 128: Leonard von Matt/Photo Researchers. 129-135: Ron Weidenhoeft/Saskia/Editorial Photocolor Archives. 136: Mauro Pucciarelli, Rome. 138-139: Giancarlo Costa, Rome. 143: Gabinetto Communale Stampe, Rome. 145-169: David Lees, Florence.

SUGGESTED READINGS

Bamm, Peter, *The Kingdoms of Christ.* Thames and Hudson, 1959.

Calvesi, Maurizio, *Treasures of the Vatican.* Editions d'Art Albert Skira, 1962.

De Campos, D. Redig, ed., *Art Treasures of the Vatican.* Prentice-Hall, Inc., 1974.

Hartt, Frederick, *History of Italian Renaissance Art.* Prentice-Hall, Inc. and Harry N. Abrams, Inc. 1969.

Haskell, Francis, *Patrons and Painters.* Yale University Press, 1980.

Hibbard, Howard, *Michelangelo: Painter, Sculptor, Architect.* The Viking Press, 1978.

Lees-Milne, James, *Saint Peter's.* Hamish Hamilton, 1967.

Mee, Charles L., Jr., *White Robe, Black Robe.* G. P. Putnam's Sons, 1972.

Pastor, Ludwig, *History of the Popes from the Close of the Middle Ages.* McGrath Publishing Co., 1978.

Pius II, Pope, *Memoirs of a Renaissance Pope, The Commentaries of Pius II.* G. P. Putnam's Sons, 1959.

Vasari, Giorgio, *The Lives of the Artists.* Penguin Books, 1965.

Walsh, Michael, *An Illustrated History of the Popes, Saint Peter to John Paul II.* St. Martin's Press, 1980.

INDEX

Page numbers in **boldface type** refer to illustrations and captions.

Roman Empire
    under Constantine, 14
    persecution of Christians in, 12
Rome
    attacked by Holy Roman Empire, 111
    barbarian attacks on, **6**, 15
    catacombs of, 13-14, **16-21**
    invaded by Saracens, 23
    papacy moved to Vatican in, 24
    Pius IX's restoration of, 144
    revolution in (1848), 140
    sacked by Germans (1527), **48**
    St. Peter's Basilica in, 47, 74-77, **75**,
        108-109, **112-117**, 120, **120-135**
    Sancta Sanctorum in, **25-41**
    Sistine Chapel in, 70, 79-80, **81-105**
Urban VIII's influence upon, 107-108,
    118
Rossellino, Bernardo, 47, 54
Rossi, Pellegrino, **138,** 140

Sacred Roman Rota, **47**
Saint Benedict's monastery (Monte
    Cassino), 22
Saint Calixtus, catacombs of, 13, **20**
St. John Lateran (Rome), 14, 142
St. Maria convent (Campo Marzio), **48**
St. Peter's Basilica (Rome), 13
    altarpieces of, **112-117**
    baldachin in, 120, **121-135**
    built under Constantine, 14
    pillaged by Saracens, 23
    Pius II and, 47
    rebuilt under Julius II, 74-77, **75**
    Urban VIII and, 108-109, **110, 120**
Saint Peter's tomb (Vatican), **6, 75,** 76
Sancta Sanctorum (Rome), **25-41**
Sangallo, Antonio da, 76
Sangallo, Giuliano da, **75,** 76
San Giussepe dei Falegnami (Rome), **140**
San Lorenzo Fuori Le Mure (Rome), 144
San Paolo Fuori Le Mure (Rome), 144
San Petronio (Bologna), 79
Santa Maria Maggiore (Rome), 144

Saracens, 23
Sardinia, 141
Scala Regia (Rome), 120
Scala Sancta (Rome), 142
Scotland, 45
Senigallia (Italy), 137
Sforza family, **78**
Shadrach (biblical), **20**
sibyls (mythology), **89-91, 96, 98, 115**
Simon (disciple), *see* Peter (saint)
Sistine Chapel (Rome)
    built by Sixtus IV, 70
    Michelangelo's ceiling for, 79-80,
        81-105
Sixtus IV (pope), 70, **83, 98**
Sixtus V (pope), **75**
Solomon (biblical), **83, 129**
spadone (sword), **146**
Spagna, Carlo, **117**
Spain
    Catholicism in, 111
    Julius II and, 73, 80
Stephen II (pope), 22, **27**
Swiss Guard, **76**
sword (spadone), **146**
Syllabus of Errors (Pius IX), 141, 143
Sylvester I (pope), **14**

Tacitus, Cornelius, 10-12
Thirty Years' War, 118
tiara (gift to Pius IX), **146-149**
Tivoli (Italy), 76
tombs
    catacombs as, 13-14, **16, 19, 20**
    of Christ, **28**
    of Julius II, 77-80, **96**
    of Saint Peter, **6, 75,** 76, 120, **123**
    relics moved to Sancta Sanctorum
        from, **27**
    of Urban VIII, **107**
Trajan (emperor, Roman Empire), 12
Trent, Council of, 111
triptychs, **50, 53**
Turks, **54,** 55, **55,** 56, **68,** 111

Urban VI (pope), 24
Urban VIII (Maffeo Barberini; pope),
    107-108, **107, 108, 110,** 111-118

baldachin of St. Peter's built under,
    120, **121, 123, 129**
Galileo and, 118-119
St. Peter's altarpieces and, **112**
St. Peter's consecrated by, 109, **120**

Valerian (emperor, Roman Empire),
    12
Vandals, 15
Vasari, Giorgio, 74, 77, **104**
Vatican
    Borgia apartments in, **78**
    Julius II and, 74-76
    mosaic of John VII in, **6**
    papacy moved from France to, 24
    sacked by Germans (1527), **48**
Vatican City State, 144
Vatican Council, First (1869), 141-142,
    142
Vatican Palace, 74, 109
    Scala Regia and, 120
Venice (Italy), 72, 73, 111
Victor Emmanuel II (king, Sardinia and
    Italy), 142
Victoria (queen, England), 140

Wars
    between England and France, 45
    between Papal States and Holy Roman
        Empire, 111
    of Papal States, under Julius II, 72-74
    Thirty Years', 118
    of Turks, **54,** 55, **55,** 56

Zechariah (biblical prophet), **98, 104**